NEW CENTURY NORTH AMERICAN POETS

Editors
John Garmon
Donna Biffar
Wayne Lanter

River King Poetry Press
Freeburg, Illinois, U.S.A.

River King Poetry Press
P.O. Box 122
Freeburg, IL 62243

Manufactured in the United States of America

Set in Times Roman and Nosfer

Cover by Smoke and Mirrors Design

Typesetting by Tom O Campbell and Donna Biffar

Special thanks to Emily A. Lambeth-Climaco
for proofing portions of the book

ISBN: 0-9650764-1-5

In memory of
Paul Dilsaver

1949-2002

Contents

i

Paul Dilsaver—1949-2002

by John Garmon

> I've moved on, old friend,
> out past the need for
> plumbing and fences,
> beyond the necessity
> of phone lines and electricity.
>
> from *Disconnected*

This anthology is dedicated to the memory of Paul Dilsaver who died on May 22, 2002. He and I first read our poems together at a public gathering in Wyoming in the early seventies. At the time we were Wyoming community college English teachers, and after leaving Wyoming we stayed in touch for thirty years.

A man dedicated to poets and poetry, writing and publishing, through the years Paul discovered many new poets, and under the imprint of his Academic & Arts Press, gave dozens of poets a launching pad. He published the first work of Yusef Komunyakaa, who went on to win the Pulitzer Prize.

Paul Dilsaver was a widely published poet, as well as a successful fiction writer. He published numerous short stories in various American magazines. His collection of short fiction, *Stories of the Strange*, appeared in 1985. A novel, *Nurtz! Nurtz!*, continues to enjoy a strong following and has taken on the stature of an underground, cult classic.

His first book of poems, *Malignant Blues*, was a collection that announced Paul as an iconoclast, a cynic, a poet whose work took bold, often sarcastic jabs at society —and at comfortable, academic poets and MFA program poetry. Over the years Paul became known as somewhat of a misanthrope and determined critic of the mainstream literary establishment. He possessed some of the characteristics of Bukowski, Ginsberg, Kerouac, Mencken, and Burroughs. In his review of *A Cure for Optimism*, in *Oyster Bay Review,* Kevin McGowin writes "Paul Dilsaver is a homeopathic practitioner of poetry . . . for Dilsaver, 'optimism' is a trite and naïve luxury we can no longer afford . . . ."

Paul's other books of poetry include: *A Brutal Blacksmith, An Anvil of Bruised Tissue, Character Scatology, Medi-Phobia, Hardcore Haiku, Book of Tears,* and a series of prose poems, *Encounters with the Anti-Christ.* He edited three anthologies, *Words Wyoming, The Toilet Papers,* and *Indicting God.* He served as editor of *Rocky Mountain Creative Arts Journal* and of *Blue Light Review.*

Eleven In the Sticks

When she was very young she'd gone down
to the spur, long discontinued then, and wished
that she could travel as she walked the ties,
then shoeless, toughening her feet against
the splintered wood the color of her Uncle Zan
when he came back from San Juan Hill, rough
riding still, and dandled her upon his knee
and handled her, and then she wished
that she could travel far from cows and daddy
crawling pie-eyed in the door at two, and Randy,
making fun of her because he had his thing
and she had none, and wished that she'd
grow bosoms soon like Cecily and Maud,
who seemed to know important things,
like how to grow a way to travel out of here.

—Earl Coleman

Busting Out

If the market don't get you then the workload will,
as you take three jobs for a thousand dollar bill,
with a broom up your ass and your guts on fire,
and your creditors nagging at the end of the wire,
and your wife's run off and your margin is due,
and your daughter's on crack, and there's no one to sue
for your fucked-up life, and your dreams of riches,
of wheels and boats and sun and stitches,
and gourmet pasta, and pears out of season,
and sinful chocolate to subvert your reason;
then it's half past quotes, and the next gig's far,
and you race to your ultimate mag wheel car,
and you tool on out, like commercials claim,
cause you need no family, joy or brain —
there's the road to love, and the power to take it,
your Beamer, your threads, to prove you could make it,
but you drive to the edge where a change is blowing,
and you pass all the malls and you keep on going,
past the smell of the oil, and the stink of the glut,
and you find yourself thinking — you could live in a hut,
at the end of nowhere, minus all this gear,
and shake off the nightmare they've dreamed up here.

—Earl Coleman

Candy Store Caper

"Wait! I'll help you with the door," old Goldstein said,
gimping his way around the candy counter. Pregnant
with my looting of his stock and petrified, back pockets
fat with Mr. Goodbar, Baby Ruth, encumbered by my
books and sack of lunch and taffy bag I'd paid two
pennies for, I was fixed, rooted to the floor by guilty feet.

I'd put them back and never steal from him again!
My teeth were a disaster anyway with all my stolen *chazerai*!
Was there a greater criminal in all of Bensonhurst?
Was there a question he would find me out?
Unless he took great pity on me I was doomed.
What would my mother say?

"Here," he smiled at me. "So little and so burdened down."
He patted me on the backside as he opened up the door,
and stopped! The telltale crinkly wrappers and the bulge
had given me away. The look he turned on me I never
saw again - until the confrontation in the car
when Marlon Brando knows he's been betrayed for years.

—Earl Coleman

Merger

Two corporate shells, we lie fully invested
in each other, unable to achieve the euphoria
of rising to all-time highs, when I was the bull,
and you Europa, with our pooled resources.

We remain uneasily Viagra-less at the fall
of the Dow, shrinking all to soon, yet even
more preoccupied with the growth of the boys
we have spun off, capable only of speculation

on the intrinsic worth of our family in this
odd-lot society. We look apprehensively
to the heavens, wary of sky wars, and try
not to view mankind as the mutual fund.

Indeed, our interest is high, as missiles rise
and fall, and Global Crossing's fiber-optics
stock sinks out of sight. We can't get out
of this market, and have no choice but total

commitment, since our family bonds might be
liquidated in some brokered exchange.
We touch, fearful of the international business
machine, afraid our dividends may be harrowing.

—Earl Coleman

saint brigids well

this spring its washed
waters its clarity of purpose
cavern cool as the night into morning
all welcomed here
those bearers of the red cloths
strips to be left for some ancient purpose
these scrawled notes and the relics
witnessing their old cures

who names this well
given saint brigid
her dubious reality
authentic as the burren
her cross over every door

anyone who comes here knows her
and for a souls ease
from the beginning of the world
a promise that has to be kept

I will say now
that this saint
wears the shawl of every woman
needing the cool purity of this
dark place
every woman used
or left by the roadside
or in some consensual joy
wherever they were or are

but I must temper the dramatics
this well belongs to all
women whoever breathed in ireland
and if there are cures in this water
the saints have tended down the years
I say how could it be otherwise

—John Knoepfle

all hallows for samhain

this is how it begins
we have purchased our candy
the porch light will be on
and the kids will come begging
the little ghosts or tramps or whatever

when there were stone houses
or in the walled hovels even
the jointstools were warm at the hearth
and the cottage doors
they were left open the night long
that fell dark when the dead came home

that was until the famine
and who was left living then
if only the walking dead
and the turf fires went cold

the dead and the living dead
who was left to whisper their names
or tell them how much she loved them

and here in illinois
it is cold and turning for winter
and tonight at the old state capitol
a political rally
where the past would come forward
this election year

well I have begun
kindled a heap of sticks
and what is it I am looking for
a place at the fire maybe

—John Knoepfle

dancing with the inupiaq

the man dancing on one foot
told us he did not know
where his songs came from
only that his grandmother sang them

we understood how it was with him
how the man at the desk and that one
skulking in the beloved fields
would tell him it did not matter

so we put on our gloves
and we all got up and danced
keeping time as well as we knew
and awkward as a room full of bears

learning how the inupiaq dance

—John Knoepfle

on flattop mountain
lines for a miscarried child

before this world
was sent spinning into the stars

before the seas
rose out of their fathoms
and knocked at the land

before the glory of starlight
and the moon that pale light
hanging in a blue sky
even into the noontime of the day

oh small wonder
quick wavering light
there in our northern lights

you were in the divine presence
and now you will be always
fixed in the palm of gods broken hand

goodbye now and goodbye
and welcome and welcome

—John Knoepfle

Two Women Leaving Beijing

We follow the evening tide that pulls
us through the railway station's
halls like seawater sucked
into caves. Dazed by the swell,
I see myself among swarms
of fish—one small neon among
swirls of dark silver. They flow

around me like chains, hauling
their burdens from earth's center
where almost everything sleeps.
We inch toward a stairwell, ooze
through its narrows, fan out wide
to a bay where black trains
fume and sigh. At last we grow

legs, walk upright, breathe.
I notice a woman hurrying beside me
the shape of my mother, dangling
a carp in mesh, its body frozen
in weather. I start to live

in her clothes. My son,
his wife and two little ones
shiver in our upstairs room,
anxious to see me thaw out
the prize, stir a white batter,
heat up the stove—but I can't

finish this scene without seeing
my own son, tall, his jaw bearded,
his blue eyes keen, grinning
beside his car with a salmon
hooked on his thumb. Just then

the woman stops, swings her fish
up the steps of the train as I pass
on to mine. She hesitates as if
I had called her and turns
at the door. We look

toward each other like migrant
women of two different tribes,
tending separate fires, clutching
our skins around us, rising to see
who comes.

—Elinor Benedict

A Daughter-In-Law Watches the Old Man Hesitate

From the kitchen window she watches Grandfather
outside, standing on top of the long wooden
stairway that leads to the lake. Bundled
in blue wool, zipped up for zero, he waits
for something to happen. But what on a day
like this, frozen from thistle to oak,
could the old man expect? Something

about the turn of his head, his leather cap's
earflaps lifted like wings, tells her
he's listening to ice. She knows the sound
from another December, the day she stood
on the stairs herself, watching the birches
lean on each other, brittle, ready to drop
their branches on snow. She'd thought then:
old bones breaking. But to Grandfather

it's probably a noise she wouldn't imagine:
Artillery. Blasting in quarries. Hunters
blamming their rifles. Woodcutters felling
the last of the white pines. Or if his mood
is milder, maybe a beaver slapping his tail
on water, or a grouse drumming his wings
for a mate. Whatever the old man thinks,

if he really goes down to the lake, he'll
hear the creak of his elbows reaming out
inches of ice with an auger; knees, knotted
and stiff, snapping with weight as he bends
to the hole with his bucket and gear.

She looks him over—bandaged, almost,
in coats and muffler, surely unable to lift
a struggling pike through a small, dark "o."
He hesitates, seems to forget where he is.
She thinks: if he were an Eskimo woman
they'd send him off on a floe. But just
as she watches him drift out to sea

he lowers his earflaps, buckles his boots,
and booms down the steps one more time.

—Elinor Benedict

Clairvoyance

*Elizabeth Newport frequently exhibited what can be
properly called clairvoyance, in which she was able
to discern the future or to reveal conditions within a
person not known to any but themselves.*
       —Memoir compiled by Ann A. Townsend, 1878

Do I believe my friend Miles when he relates
his dream—the one interrupted
by his wife's call to come look at the news,
just in time to see the second plane
hit the tower and the flames roiling away,
grey smoke shrouding some of it—the death
within? As the towers collapsed
Miles and Mary stood in their living room
and saw a few victims leaping out windows
before the TV producers decided
This is too much, even for us.

Damned right I believe him—Miles
my friend and tai chi teacher and vet
of Vietnam. In the dream he had stood
high in a skyscraper, peering out through
a window taped in black except for a slot
like that in a tank or a helmet. He gazed
down upon both towers and the Empire
State Building. And although he knew
even in the dream that the perspective
was all wrong, he thought nothing of it.
Next to him two men were chatting—
"young middle-eastern men."

Although they were not speaking in English,
Miles is still trying to recover what
they said just before he awoke to see
what the rest of us saw—he and his wife
in their living room, I and my wife
standing in ours as we said: This must
be a movie, not the news. It's just
a mix-up on Channel Four—but also
on Nine and Thirteen. We did not
check Sesame Street as we began to weep.

My friend Miles would never lie
and I've had enough odd events in my life
to know they can happen—the clairvoyant,
the telepathic, the never explainable.
Death opens the door for such glimpses
into other worlds. But soon such a witness
as Miles betrays the gift he has been given,
begins to apologize, say "You must think
I am nuts." They work hard to convince
themselves that the dream was only a dream,
nothing more. But the nightmare is what
they awake to, not what they dream.

—David Ray

Preparing the Monument

They are hard at work on a monument
while the smoke is still roiling out of the pit,

raising the question of how much effort
it takes to pound the present into the past

and quickly convert a disaster still in progress
to the status of an ancient and archaic attraction.

They have chosen a fire truck mangled and twisted
to set on a plinth, along with a few smashed cars.

They are extracting relics not yet gone cold
and unearthing what is already entombed.

Though the dust has not settled and the smoke
is still noxious in nostrils they are braving

fouled air to assemble debris, and have applied
for permission to choose an unknown victim

to be interred in salvaged aluminum. For any
design calling for names stamped in bricks, tiles,

frieze or entablature they have been given a list.
Once their monument, centered on a smooth terrace

with a few tasteful trees, is in place they can gaze
upon this space called ground zero and not be blinded

or overcome by the stench, and when their work
is complete and every surface polished and gleaming

and ready for tourists, they themselves will be free
of fear, as if they are dealing only with the archaic—

desiccate, bloodless, and cold, with no smoke
in the air, and no catastrophe in progress. Once

I too sought out the archaic and found it on an island
in Greece, a fragment in marble that had once

been the foot of a lion, but he was already a thing
of the past and I did not have to chase him there.

As for the present, Buddha said it well—everything
is burning—everything, nothing not burning—

and to enshrine the flames is hardly a task
                              for mere mortals.

—David Ray

The Neighborhood of Saint Jude
Managua, Nicaragua

The barrio

In the neighborhood of San Judas
there's always something
going on down the street.
Even the trees lean over the walls
so as not to miss anything.

Morning rush hour is people walking downhill
on sloping dirt streets,
some dressed smartly like Jenny's
daughter-in-law Diana who
works at RentaCar,
some in threadbare slacks and shirts
for a day of hard labor,
some carrying jars or buckets on their heads,
stopping for a chat with neighbors.

You can shop at the Pulperìa—
San Judas's 7-11.
The woman who owns the Pulperìa says,
"You are so happy. Here we are suffering.
Here we have nothing."
Behind her are empty boxes.
She has little left to sell.
One room in her house is completely empty.
She has sold everything in it
to get money.

In San Judas worlds coexist.
A dude on a sleek new motorcycle
inches down the street slowly slowly,
so the girls can admire his chrome.

Two oxen pull a wooden-wheeled wagon
full of firewood.
A pack of long-legged dogs
with tall ears and emaciated bellies
noses along the wall for food.

In the evening teenagers come out.
They stand in doorways in groups.
The girls have style. The boys are
handsome and dangerous.
A boy and girl walk down the road holding hands.
The barrio shimmers with energy.
Eros and agape.

At night the banana trees sleep,
masses of shadow.
The cats wake up.
You listen in the sweaty dark
to engines revving and backfiring,
cattle lowing, radios playing
meringue, salsa, rock 'n roll.
Sometimes you hear gun shots.
Towards morning birds sing,
Something runs, probably a cat,
across the roof.
Rain on a tin roof—first it patters,
then it thrums.
Wind rushes through the room.
Water patters on the windowsill.
It smells clean,
a baptism, a visitation of grace.
A thousand roosters crow the sun up.

Jenny

I stay with you.
You cook me red beans and rice and fried bananas.
I take your photograph
in front of the Republic of Panama School
where you
teach first grade for $35 a month—
which is not enough, even in Nicaragua
to support a family.

In the time of the revolution, you tell me,
things were better. Now
the schools do not get the things they need.
There are no chairs for the children to sit on.
Books are scarce. Chalk is scarce.
"The pieces of chalk are so tiny.
They hurt my fingers
when I try to write on the blackboard."

In a spiral notebook
covered with thin, white paper
you write your poems,
dating each entry.
One honors Carlos Fonseca.
Others speak of the struggle that
must continue and of teachers
and how they too must continue
in spite of difficulties
educating the young.

You also write about love—
"I was born strong.
I lived strong,
but I was not so strong
the day I met you."

Clothes Hanging on a Line

Clothes hanging on a line
make a rainbow in San Judas,
but they have a story to tell.

You buy them in little shops.
They are called American clothes.
They come from the United States.
They are second hand clothes, clothes the
big retailers couldn't sell,
clothes you and I sent to Goodwill.
They are packed into containers
and shipped on freighters to
Nicaragua, Haiti, Honduras—
wherever people are poor.
And this is called—free trade.

The odd thing is that some of these clothes
might have been sewed together by
Nicaraguans working in sweatshops
right here in the Free Trade Zone.
But they're definitely not for sale
at the point of manufacture.

Well, how could a woman afford a
$20 shirt that she made
for 13 cents?
Plus she gets searched at the door
to be sure she hasn't stolen any—
American clothes.

—Peggy Sower Knoepfle

Snow Lake

We might have guessed its cunning,
having to crack its steely mirror
each time we waded in.
Yet, growing up beside it,
we saw in it
only our own silvery world.
When it drowned Sammy Erickson,
keeping to this day
his bones,
we still did not comprehend
and laid our blankets down
and built our small fires and counted stars.
We ignored the razors of glass
nightly sharpening themselves along the shore,
the stuttering codes
glinting off the water.
Sunsets, white sails, our young bodies
obscured the docks' slow rot,
stumps rising under speeding boats
like sharks,
the bones of Sammy Erickson
turning the wrong way home.

—Jo McDougall

21

At Mercy Hospital

My daughter lies in the last stage
of her disease.
Making my way to her room,
I meet a gurney, empty I assume,
until I see the small rise
in the covering sheet.
I know a body is there,
or what's left of one.

Entering her room,
my fears rage like dreams:
Where is the doctor?
Where is the priest?
What are they doing with that sheet?

—Jo McDougall

In Due Time

The vet has removed the cat's infected molars
and left him to his bliss.
Finally home, we lay him on his claw-ravaged rug
and build a fireplacc fire.
Slowly, dreaming his way,
he inclines his face to the hearth
to warm the empty spaces inside.

Like one of Ebenezer's ghosts,
my father in his wheelchair in the sun
of a faraway Arkansas August lawn
shimmers along the ceiling.
Shrunk to bone by the blossoming cancers,
he shivers himself warm.

Afflictions. Little mercies.
Cat, this fire's the best we have to offer
to atone.
Father, the blankets were plentiful but thin
and never did much good.

The cat tries to stand.
The floor has turned to jello and they've moved the walls.
He will sleep through today and tomorrow. Then the pain,
then food and naps in his own time,
the front step then to linger, then the yard
where he will be his old self
as the vet has promised,
although no longer able to break
the important bones of birds.

—Jo McDougall

The Wait

A buzzard riding the thermals
above a pine beside a Louisiana highway
spots the carcass of a small dog
left by a speeding car.
It is mid-July. A gossamer of trembling
alerts the buzzard's spine.
Here is an odor with promise.
Soon the air will turn to an oily shimmer,
a texture of such velvet and exquisite heft
that the buzzard contents himself to wait,
rocking night after night in the arms of the pine.

—Jo McDougall

Into Dusk

An old farm house slides
into dusk. Quietly.
Fading into a windbreak.
Its paint grays to fog.

Window frames sag, the way
the eyes of the old, who
having outlived their loves,
stare at a point behind you.

Wall boards sigh as they
warp away from the frame,
gradually easing out nails
against their cries.

Floors whisper of the past
to anyone who will listen
— of childhood's laughter
filling these silent rooms.

Footsteps and conversation,
now mere faltering echoes
trapped in spider webs,
dust, and broken mirrors.

Lean close to hear
what decay recalls
in unhinged syllables
and fragmented grammar.

Don't shrink back
from the musty air
of its murmuring voice.
Its story may be yours.

—Charles Levendosky

Burden of War

I.

Artillery observer on the front lines,
Dad didn't talk much about what he saw
after he returned from Korea decorated
and disjointed — his eyes still focused
on what they had witnessed there.
He could not comprehend, nor could we.

Had been far enough North to see Chinese
"hordes," he called them, cross the border,
to hear their war cries and battle horns
as they charged. He confessed to us once:
"The clamor could turn a brave man's blood
to jelly. Worse than anyone can imagine."

Lost his young Jeep driver to a land mine.
When drinking heavily, Dad would sometimes
mimic the sound of the explosion, "whump"
and shake his head, his eyes in that place.
Bottle after bottle contained tiny explosions
that dulled those memories — year upon year.

II.

This story, then, from a fellow officer:
"An old woman with a child behind her were
walking toward your old man. She held out
a hand, begging for food. Your father dug
in his jacket to find something to offer.
She bent at the waist. I just came around

the corner in time. Granny had an automatic
rifle strapped on her back. It was pointed
at your father. The boy — half your age —
reached for the trigger. I shot them both.
First the boy, then his old mamasan.
Strange war, women and kids trying to kill us."

III.

I can only guess now that my father carried
them for the rest of his days. Digging down
into himself, into whiskey stupor. Each drink
proved he was still willing to offer food or aid,
unwitting beneficiary of that terrible trade
— two lives for his, a child and a grandmother.

—Charles Levendosky

Love's Epiphanies

I.

You push two fingers into a knot of pain
below your shoulder, "There," you whisper.

Where my thumb presses, I feel a tiny fist
slowly open and release some old anguish
you gathered before we met. With my touch
I push it back into the past.

It will return, but I will be here
to unclench it. Open all our hands.

II.

When we kiss after we have made love,
little animal noises issue from my throat.
I am singing into you. This joy, into you.

—Charles Levendosky

The Forest Park Zoo Caper

Not a soul would have guessed
he was casing a job.
A local of little note,
he slouched in the pipe-lined alley
that kept a curious crowd
from crushing the elephant.

For people came in waves,
drawn by a vague faith
in the large and foreign,
to throng before the bare patch
where the paunchy exile paced
and baked in the Texas sun.

Hanging loose in the shade
laid by vaulting oaks,
the squirrel just bided his time.
Pure cool, the russet hustler
hid a sprinter's coil
beneath his fuzzy coveralls.

Meanwhile, the elephant shuffled,
doing his act for peanuts.
To each offered morsel,
he'd loll and flop his trunk
as if in supreme effort,
and the lookers lapped it up.

Finally a child's frail hand,
trembling forward, flinched
from the hot wet breath
and let a nut plummet.
It tumbled to the concrete
near the lazily flailing shadow.

In the split-instant of the miss,
the thief shucked his cover
and became a violent rusty blur
that streaked beneath the pipes
with the speed of a cheetah,
the flair of Errol Flynn.

He seized the nut on a short hop
with no hitch in stride,
even when the lumpy trunk
mustered one frantic lash
that bumped his bottle-brush tail.
Unflustered, the squirrel curved

to scurry broken-field
through the thicket of legs,
then darted railroad-straight
across the shimmering sidewalk,
underneath a green bench and on,
finally scrambling up a skinny elm.

There he stopped at last:
Against pale sapphire sky,
he reared in a sun-drenched fork
and hoisted his haul
with tan-gloved hands.
Safe in his lofty element

of leaves and air and light,
oblivious of the gawking crowd
he'd also captured, the furry raider
ripped through the peanut's hull
and crunched into the meat
with diamond-like incisors.

And even as he chewed,
a raucous brassy chatter
blared from his fanning jaws
to echo throughout the zoo
and stir caged cats, disturb
dull dreamers in the ape house.

—Tony Clark

My Wife Among the Apaches

A dreadful note jarred Linda from sleep
one night when she lived at San Carlos.
Peering out a window, she saw
in her porch light's stark aura
a small gray owl perched
on a branch of thorny mesquite.
With round eyes locked
on hers, it hooted once more.

On the Rez, according to her students,
the owl's a foreteller of death.
At school next day, Linda made haste
to question a colleague who would know.

The woman frowned at first,
then a shy smile shaped her auburn face
and her coal-dark eyes grew bright.
You don't need to worry, she said:
When the owl brings that kind
of news, it will speak Apache.

—Tony Clark

Dreaming My Grandfather's Dreams
Suldal Valley, Norway 1998

My grandfather slept in this farmhouse
as a child. Here, this night,
grandfather many times over,
I lie in the very same first home
of the grandfather I never knew,
who died before I could know
a father could have a father.

In mountain darkness I listen
to the silence of the house,
first room hammered square
two and a half centuries past,
beams hand-hewn, timber
from steep slopes eavesdropping now,
the house expanded by generations
coming down the centuries
like logs from the mountainside,
farm name and family name the same.

In the house of my father's father,
where this mountain stillness
tucked round him like a quilt,
I drift off to sleep,
dream ancestral dreams —
cold dreams of stone fences,
warm dreams of evening lamps
and dinner table din;
gentle dreams of cows,
neck bells clinking them
home for milking time,
plashy dreams of silvery salmon

finning the Suldal River
from the sea to spawn
(I imagine I hear the water
move through the dark).

In the house of his childhood
I dream my grandfather's dreams
and I am a child as well.
An ocean removed from home
in a country I have never seen,
wrapped in the comforter
of my history, I dream
my grandfather's dreams.

—Glen Sorestad

Kvikne in Rain

Rain pelts us as we drive
along mountainside so sheer
I imagine a sheep losing its footing,
pitched like a boulder from a precipice
to the winding Lagan River below.
I peer at this jagged vertical world,
the valley known as Gudbrandsdal,
where grassy pastures clamber
up from the valley floor.
I try to imagine my grandfather,
Ellend Lien, born here amid
sheep bleat and cattle bawl,
born beneath the overhang
of brooding mountains whose names
are unknown to me; try to imagine
the stunned shock in his eyes,
having travelled half a world
from this pinched valley
to a mind-bending horizon
of sprawling prairie grasslands.

In the village of Kvikne we stop
beside the heavy-timbered church
erected before a single place of worship
had been raised in the land
my grandfather chose. We walk
the graveyard, close beneath our umbrella,
listen to percussive drops on fabric,
the swish of our feet in wet grass,
the crunch of shoes on crushed rock,
the cry of a wet rook from its perch.

We walk past rows of headstones,
centuries of farming folk who picked
their way with care behind their animals
in this pastoral world of up and down.

With each gravestone name I utter,
I mouth my history;
with each cold touch of wet marble,
my fingers invoke something
I can not know, but feel
and therefore trust,
though I can not even now
establish all connections.
History carved in stone:
this graveyard, a country I have
never seen before, but feel—
some newly discovered part of me.

—Glen Sorestad

Watching Her Die
For J.W.

We spend the afternoon on small talk,
shopping for small things,
hunger's quick fix, something brief
to placate exhaustion from long hours on call.
I watch his face as he watches shoppers,
looking for tell-tale signs of health.
Side-by-side two women, obese, in black spandex,
crowd us, filling their carts.
"That's what I see in clinic," he says,
"everyday. Mostly from the Midwest.
It's what they eat, a lack of self-awareness."

And almost as an afterthought,
"I have a patient," he tells me,
offering a litany of medical terms,
a haze of symptoms,
that beyond the signs
of an organism struggling to stay alive,
have little to do with bad habits.
Bipolar, high fever, acidic blood,
platelets clotting, a series of microscopic
log-jams at the center of the torrent.
Her blood thinned enough to leak away at random.
 "We've tried everything," he says.
"Nothing fits."

Nothing fits—small things
that should add up are shrouded in mist,
even beneath the bright eye of science,
small things that evade the sight
and insight connections of his inner senses.
My failure to anticipate his words.
"I'm going to lose her."

The women push off.
In front of us the aisle is empty,
all the way down.
"This will be the first," he says.
"And she's only thirty."

But the afternoon is warm and breezy,
the parking lot aflood with busy people
at float on an improbity of soft light
painting the genetic stream
with inevitable degeneration.

Resigned to insolvency
seeking salvation,
on an otherwise sunny day,
the impossibilities of altering
the flow, to relieve our hunger, even
briefly, I ride beside a somber man
who all his life has said
that what he wanted most
was to help someone.

The following day his brother calls
to pass to me an anonymous,
universal sort of grief, saying,
"he called to let you know,
the woman he was talking about,
died last night."

—Wayne Lanter

Counseling the Children

My pose is prayer but yet my head is filled
With the terrifying dissonances of God.
　　　　　　　　　　　—Peter Porter
　　　　　　　"The Last Hours of Cassiodorus"

　　　　　　　I write this to update you on the tragedy
　　　　　　　of Monday. During the evening hours
　　　　　　　a student's parent took her life.

What there was of family is now rent,
a woman dead, a mother gone. Her children
heard the shot. All three of them, like living
in a fairy tale. Someone to blow the house down.

　　　　　　　Our condolences to the bereaved
　　　　　　　and their friends. We are concerned
　　　　　　　with our students at this difficult time.

They heard the argument and then the shot,
but not the voices all the years before,
the lies that lead to a dissolution of ties.
But what they heard is now of no import.

　　　　　　　These kind of things leave scars
　　　　　　　we can alleviate or prevent by giving
　　　　　　　everyone additional support.

You simply can not talk them out of this.
They will insist that people die who have lived.
There's nothing to do but huddle down against the wind.
Yes, tell them anger is acceptable. It always is.

A crisis intervention team came in
today to help our school family
get through this time of difficulty.

But there is no family here. And if they're scared,
well, so are we. Tell them it is unfortunate
that humans have to witness such a thing. Assure
them their sense of pain and loss is natural as rain.

They have specialists who can
relate to those who will not adjust
or need additional future support.

And yes, tell them they're at fault, for loving
even the sorry parts of life. But do not tell
them there is tragedy in this. Soft words
will not assuage their grief or dispel fear.

If anyone feels they need to talk
about this tragedy, contact our office
for counseling at this difficult time.

And by the way, in the end, be sure to say how
even good arrangements come apart. So, if you will,
hate yourself, but do not point to those who tell you
that what is can not be changed or rearranged.

—Wayne Lanter

Something Like Those Mice
for Bryan

A soldier on the news said
he knows how to deal with war, snipers
and explosions, but he doesn't know
how to deal with after. Sometimes,
the uncommon is common. Everything pushes
the limits. Like the Western edge
of Eastern time, where, in summer,
it's daylight until 10 p.m.

There are no guarantees
I tell myself. Still,
if the body were more glenoid,
more like a spoon's bowl,
maybe it could catch and hold light
so I could scrutinize it
and find out if, inside an egg,
light shrivels to the kind of near-dark
that makes me want to rent a video,

a foreign one injected with music
that says more than subtitles,
so I can close my eyes and ignore
the dark print on pamphlets that read
"Abdominal pain. . .changes in bowel habits. . ."
But, hell, you'd said, *yesterday's Szechuan pork,*
last Sunday's prime rib. . .
it all comes back differently,

Last year, you slit a pig's throat
and caught it's blood in a kettle
while I sat on the shed floor
after vomiting. Thirsty.
Thinking about those desert mice
that come out at dawn
to lick water from stones.

Is there a theme to any of this?
Maybe how a root becomes a tree that rots
and falls down its own center,
or how a giant water bug
turns a frog's insides to juice
then sucks it down to a crumpled skin?
And is everything about appetite?
About eating and being eaten?

I wanted to yell, *Chew back!*
Instead, I watched bees bump against
a once-open gap between the walls,
bouncing off a caulk seal I'd laid,
my head covered with cheesecloth
as if it could keep all of me unstung.

And, despite my usual trust
in things like Our Maker,
or tags that read "Safety Approved,"
lately I've been up at dawn
in search of one of those
it's-right-there-in-front-of-you miracles,
something like those mice,
and the water from stones.

—Anne Ohman Youngs

Wild Horse Adoption

For 15 minutes I watch him,
a dapple gray who froths and bucks
as if trying to dislodge the consequences
of my imagination: fences, sugar cubes,
a belief I can ease him by rubbing
something called love into his flanks
and whispering, *It's all right,*
the way, when I was 6, my mother used to rub
Vicks into my chest, saying,
By morning you'll be fine,

but first the tossing and sweating
to douse the fever.
Maybe the gray's bared-teeth-lunges
are like those fevers, just temporary
power surges, or Dakota plains aberrations
slow to fizzle out and leave him
easy as apples, those late October ones,
sweet after the first frost.
Then maybe I wouldn't expect so much,
just apple flavor

instead of this never-ending chase
after some unnamed, untamed desire
that will, more than likely, end up
a waste of time, like those hours I spend
watching moonlight slash fences
and slice trees, always headed away from
but tied to where it begins.
Eyes knotted, shoulders stiff, a guy
leans over the high wooden chute and dangles
a loop above someone's far-fetched dream,

then a sharp *thwup,* as leather stings
the neck of a horse who screams language
we use when there's nothing left but adrenaline
charging the air. Consolation?
Maybe there isn't any,
maybe everything's gesture, agitated,
the swash and buckle of the men
separating the horses, snapping
white flags and shouting
as if they could transform beauty

into something more beautiful,
like spinning straw into gold, or kissing
all sleeping princesses awake.
I can see, even at a distance, the gray's
patchy winter coat, his wild eyes a story
old as petroglyphs
from some long-ago time without walls
or a floor dotted with empty Copenhagen tins,
just space and familiar smells
soothing whatever's hostile.

—Anne Ohman Youngs

over and again you see them at the pool

over and again you see them at the pool
the somewhat retarded ones
they frolic about at the children's end
their caretakers watching out for them

and frequently it strikes you
that there seems no cunning in them
sometimes you feel more akin to them
than to the others

their tentative steps
into the jacuzzi
the hot water puzzles
and frightens them at first
how it works a bit beyond their ken,
once immersed though
they seem to grasp this laving warmth

but why then does even some average of intelligence
lead invariably to a cunning
and perhaps some mean-spiritedness as well

for you—to struggle your whole life
for a bare minimum of it
some sort of vulnerability
that had a terrible time growing a false face

you remember Primo Levi writing
that the best didn't survive the camps
the ones like him that lived to testify
blemished by some spurt of cunning
that carried them through in the end
these best and the "least" linking up?

looking back on the maelstrom of your life
it always amazes you
that you lived

the official world always posed against the individual—
for you it was only through your friends
giving a hand, more than a hand
even then you barely made it over the bar
some might say not even that
perhaps you were like some idiot savant
more idiot
but then when do you come full-blown

into silence, cunning, and exile?
exile the most profoundly true
cunning slow to develop
silence always the most problematic
how to get through to the others
like Pavese said
that's the most important thing, not so?
yet finally they force the muzzle of silence over our faces

most often the ones they bring here are fairly young
but now comes an older one
nearly my age
at first you almost don't capiche
that he's one of them
his face crusted over slightly with age
with that planet of the apes masklike quality almost normal
but then you see the troubled innocence and puzzlement in
his eyes
and he keeps looking at you
as though recognizing a brother
yes—*"mon frère*
mon semblable"

—Chuck Miller

mon frère mon semblable—my brother, my double
                                        —Baudelaire

extra virgin

having a little more "bread" now
we reach for the "extra virgin" olive oil
yes, yes, cold pressed and all the rest
but more than that
it's time we are redeemed
made whole again
against this immutable corrosion
and so we reach
for some stored up sunshine's essence
ah! how good it could be
at least in our somewhat cracked psyches
to lave our worn out souls
in a bit of this extravirginity,
this green-golden fruited oil
from the "cradle of our civ"
dusky maidens and naiads
few of which we've ever seen
"only Euclid has looked on beauty bare," etc.

nonetheless we're forced to smile at the fabric of our self-deception
still attempting
in our fumbling and laughable way
to begin again
and rediscover at some too late state
some strange innocence
which has always eluded us
or perhaps that we once actually possessed
but is so deeply submerged now
that only some last estranged part of us
might know the whereabouts
of this far buried sunbathed mine
like a kingdom at the center of the earth

so we geezers, gaffers, duffers
mate with some sweet extra virgin
in the spawning ground
of our dreams' headwaters

—Chuck Miller

Time

for Kjell Askildsen

reading a Norwegian
some drama of a remote lighthouse-keeper's island
your memory opens back
and you recall lying on the floor in your late adolescence
the Sunday paper had an article on the death-bed remarks
of the literary and notable
you had asked your father what his might be
he replied without blinking
"now the farce is done"
and went back to his own perusal
surprised, you felt a kinship for him then
perhaps not so different after all

all these years later
without having properly thought of it for decades
you remember
only now, having almost lived your life
has more complex resonance
not less true
and a sort of muffled regret
only a faint and obscure hope to set against it
for then it was a protest and a premonition
at what since childhood had begun to swallow you up—
you hadn't lived through the clattering and wrenching years
which, when they let you up for air,
having gained some strength and purpose,
you struggled it to a standstill
only for brief moments

but thinking of it now
good for a rueful smile
and a bleak sense of how it rings

—Chuck Miller

Counting the Bats
For Chuck and Carolyn

Dark scraps of the chimney break away, fly off
for the night shift, while from the driveway
my neighbors count—twenty-one bats out tonight—
and wonder why their house is chosen.

Their three-story cave is colonized by winged strangers
squatting among attic treasures, the suspension
of threat hung in daytime like wet gloves from clothes pegs,
squatters who would pay their rent with guano.

If they bring their relatives, stay a century or two,
they'll fill the granary attic to the rafters with guano harvest.
Counting the bats out for night hunting reminds me
of my parents counting the small planes that droned

overhead on wartime missions, checking again
those that returned in formation or straggled back, sputtering
low over elms. When the bats next door return before dawn,
do they squeeze into my neighbors' waking dreams?

The attic door is sealed against tiny scratching shrieks,
shadows that might slide through a keyhole, like secrets.

—Judy Ray

Nights In Unfamiliar Places: IV
Visiting a Maori Marae, South Island, New Zealand

Before we set foot on the *marae* there must be a call of welcome
and one among us must respond with the Maori chant: "Please
keep calling, that we may follow your voice and not be lost."
A woman wails the welcome, stepping backwards, beckoning,
then pauses, hand fluttering at her side like a little bird. Thus
we are guided on to the *marae* where headman and elders wait.

A gift is tossed and picked up. What happened those first times,
if the chanting, tossing, stepping forward unbidden, prancing
with tongues out was a misunderstood challenge?
But for us the welcome begins, long receiving line for the *hongi*,
nose-to-nose greeting of one and all. Then the feast—heaps of lamb,
abalone gleaned from the harbor, vegetables, salad with mussels,

and plum crumble. We settle on mattresses spread around
the great hall. Tradition leads us again as each person gives
Greetings, greetings, greetings to all, that sounds like
Tenekatu, tenekatu, tenekatu to kai. My name is. . .my family is. . .
I come from. . .my river is. . .Such is my mountain. And what
brought us to this island, this peninsula, this *marae*.

Around midnight we sleep, and sometimes wake to the chorus
of snores in both Maori and English, chorus that does not diminish
the entire night. I regulate my breathing to the loudest
which come from the elder hostess who lies with her long hair wild
on the pillow. Next to this hall stands the meetinghouse,
place for discussion or disputes. And also for release, we are told.

"In there you lay down everything. Your ancestors are there,
your community, your belief. Leave the bad inside, take only good."
But I could leave nothing there, for the meetinghouse is *tapu,*
taboo to women, for which there is a faint apology from our hosts.
In formal farewell we speak from a silent circle "as the spirit moves."
The headman, in rumbling, growly voice, thanks us for our visit:

"It is good to see you come. And it is good to see you go."

—Judy Ray

Ghazal

for David Leon (born 4/21/01)

Lifting the light, clouds tower above clear unseeing eyes.
Let me introduce you, infant with clear unseeing eyes.

What focus can be found in opaque, uncensored darkness?
The halo, the aureole attracts near unseeing eyes.

A scrim, though filmy as innocence, hints at mystery.
Let us lullaby to sleep the weary unseeing eyes.

Our ancient tribes, our modern brothers—we know, but disown.
At the borders, ignorance meets fear in unseeing eyes.

Protect our future, fragile as a baby's fontanel.
The seventh generation needs a seer's far-seeing eyes.

—Judy Ray

In the North Woods

Sharing birthdays on Hemingway's 100th,
out-breathing him by two,

you swim back, forth, flexing
no waves in the cold blue,

a fish leaps, one lone ripple ring
by the island,

the rusted lifeguard mount sits in weeds
like a child's discarded highchair,

here, says the sign, Tom Welch drowned
on his 18th.

Walking home, you choose
a handful of purple phlox,

this water, this sky.

—Mary Sue Koeppel

Echoes

and everywhere
The ceremony of innocence is drowned.
—W. B. Yeats

You tasted the night,
held the wind down
deep in your throat because
now so few answers
get into your words.

Lawnmowers echo each
other like kids on a swing
calling past, up and down,
a rhythmic monotone.

Your languor is like the lawnmower
in a long figure eight around the spruce
then under the crab apple tree.
Over and over, wider and wider.

In the attic last night
you read in your ten-year-old hand:
"Dad killed Michael's rabbit yesterday.
He cried all night."
Forty years ago, why did a father kill
a seven-year-old's rabbit? Drive a hatchet
straight through the neck?
Serve that meat that Sunday dinner?
Make that boy eat?

They empty you, these questions.
You listen to the church bells, nineteen bongs.
Your father donated those echoes.

What if Michael, years later, under blue welts
had grabbed that whip?
Better to feel welts that faded to
spiked flowers on back muscles
than to be the boy grabbing his father's shirt,
fisting him to the porch floor,
sitting on his chest all through
the heart attack
if, later, a judge would call the boy—killer;
the defense—insane.

Instead, now you step into the shovel,
pull up black earth
where the evergreen your father planted
is just old roots. You pull roots out,
sweating and burning. Then
you mix calf manure with water,
pat the mixture as he taught you.
Next year will find a maple, here,
not an evergreen.

A chipmunk runs into the peonies,
swallows call into the wind,
a dove coos behind the garden shed.
Church bells bong. And
night, carefully, comes.

—Mary Sue Koeppel

Valentine's Day—Straight Up

Afterwards, she smelled
of winter just ten percent,
spring ninety percent.
The rest of us stuck in winter
breathed deeply and wished
we had lain on the pine needles
and jerked straight up from the waist,
one, two, three times she said.

We wanted even the pine cones and ants
and the rain on blond hair.
We practiced lying and jerking up
a whole body at a time, but
it didn't equal weightlessness,
the zero gravity when a lover circles.

—Mary Sue Koeppel

The Ice Cream Vigils

Whitman managed to get hold of ten gallons of
ice cream, which he personally dispensed to the
patients at Carver Hospital.
                                    —Roy Morris, Jr.
                                    The Better Angel

Ice cream for a soldier, whether North or South.
Dispense it quickly, while it's at its best.
A spoon at a time, death melts in the mouth.

It's cold enough to make you catch your breath.
For some westerners, this was their first taste
of ice cream, the flavor neither North nor South,

perfect to smooth a battle's aftermath.
The war's real story—ask the seasoned journalist
from Brooklyn—melted spoon by spoon in the mouth,

a frozen treat become the whole of truth
while it was going down. How could it last
in June, in Washington, the winds warm from the south?

To serve mere boys who'd served away their youth,
Walt Whitman crossed the capital in haste
lest there be nothing left to melt in the mouth.

Ice-cream communion, lips parted in faith, and the inclined
head of a volunteer pagan priest—
scenario for healing North and South
a spoon at a time. Death melts in the mouth.

—Philip Dacey

Doozy

Is it spelled doozy or -ey or -ie?
—from a letter

It's doozy in the dictionary, and doozy in my heart,
and doozy up and down the street.

It's doozy where the daisies roam
and dizzy where the lovers doze
and days are lazy.

It's doozy where it's Dacey
and acey-deucy upsy-daisy,
dipsy-doodle when it's crazy,
but doozy all the time.

It's doozy any way you spell it,
but dicey if you try to sell it,
doozy any way you slice it,
with doozy you don't have to spice it up.

So doozy this and doozy that
and keep your doozy hot
and let your doozy out when it wants out,

for hunky dory introibo ad altare dei
makes a fellow woozy
onesy-twosy
does he does she
yes they doozy
to the tune of Tommy Dorsey William Basie any
bluesy band.

Then tell your Suzie there's no time for choosy
and it's all good newsy
till the boozy blowsy
easy jazzy
doozy end.

—Philip Dacey

Four Hands

As I watch the handsome elderly couple
play Brahms waltzes for four hands,
the woman all flair, her body arched and swaying,
the man composed but strong of attack,
the two a long-married complement,

I wonder if the obvious positive
charge between them—hands timed
to exhilarating perfection, even
crossing, with no room for error,
like Rogers and Astaire—ever translates

into the sexual, so that more than once
they have felt compelled to bring complete
closure to a practice session (or even
recital, as now, exchanged sparkling glances
a sign of what they cannot act on, or out)

by rushing from the piano bench
into the bedroom and there, with a fumbling
of fingers not to be seen on ivory—
the buttons all uncooperative, all
tin ear—falling upon each other

like a cascade of notes, four-hand piano
a kind of foreplay, as good a fountain
of youth as one could want, Brahms only
the penultimate pleasure, the meal
before the dessert, although of course

it would be Brahms again, the couple's
joke, the fingers now playing out the score
on each other's flesh—*we must perfect this,*
we must perfect that, practice, practice—
and humming the while, until a beautiful confusion

is their reward: recital, practice,
love, music, Brahms, each other,
early years, late years, all the boundaries
washed away in a flood of intimacy,
near dizziness—say from not age

but ecstasy?—a grand union the motif
transposed into whispers
across wrinkled hands that entwine,
if you arpeggio me, I'll legato you,
or, softer, *Brahms me, Love, Brahms me again.*

—Philip Dacey

Mulberries

There are four separate reds
to each cluster: a tiny fist of pink
holding tight to the last finger
of May; then a skinned-knee red
all watery with tears; then
a flame-filled burgundy
that stains the lips; and at last
that rich shadowy red that looks
sweetly back, and from which
comes the best jelly of all.

—Ted Kooser

Moon Ants

Their caravans travel at night when the counter tops are cool
and their black djellabas blend with the shadows.
They pass the temple of the ant trap, its doors thrown open
to all four winds, but they prefer their godless ways—
the drunken welcome at camp the next morning,
the passing around of the booty, the fabulous lies:
tales of the pool of oil they discovered and drank from,
the pyramid of sweetness that sparkled with stars.

—Ted Kooser

In The Mall

The middle-school girls are practicing
their laughs, loud as shots
in front of The Gap, then again
in front of The Limited.
Their heads are still so small and perfect,
their teeth so even and white,
their hands so lacking in character,
that the gray man in his running suit,
working so hard to walk off a blue bruise
on the side of his heart,
hurts all the more for seeing them.

—Ted Kooser

No Bottom

On a raft of fenceposts roped together
and braced with scrap two-by-fours
we tipped out onto the springy skin
between us and so dark and deep a pool
my father said it had no bottom,
said it was so cold below that a body
would never decay, would never form gases
and float to the surface. We were told
a boy was down there somewhere still,
nameless, eyes open, suspended in time.
That hot summer day at the gravel pit
the four of us stood each to a corner
and laughing and daring rocked that raft
till the water splashed over our feet
and the deck grew slick, but a blue hand
reached up from below and with a puckered,
pointed finger held up the center and kept us
from turning it over, Danny, Billy,
David and I, who at twelve had not yet
been chosen to slip beneath the surface
and into the chill of examples. Now
in our sixties, separated by hundreds of miles,
each of us trembles on a craft of his own.

—Ted Kooser

Firewatch:
Wolf Creek Mountain

"That old whore's gonna get my ass, someday,"
the back of Jake's hand
rubbed across the leaping horizon
as though he were trying
to rub the fire out.
"Gonna come right down
and bite my butt."

Little Willy nodded
as he always did
when Jake's voice flared.

For about half a breath,
high up on a ridge
a geyser   of sparks
hung like a flickering umbrella
against the black.

Higher still,
the rattle of an exploding tree
slapped
down
the switchbacks
until it flattened onto the valley floor.

"Jeezuz!" Jake jerked awake
staring into Willy's Eddy Cantor face
glistening in the fire's light.
"Man can't sleep
with all that humpin'
on the ridge."

Little Willy nodded.

Diamonds the color of autumn sunsets
glittered in a tiara of beaded sweat
then grooved grey trails
through the charcoal on his cheeks.

While the night wind shook the sky,
tiny airborne fires diminished,
went out
and, for a moment,
there was nothing
for Jake or Willy to see.

In that fixed black
they heard what they had been missing.
Digging down through the depths
of the mountain's other canyon,
the fire was feeding itself again
becoming hotter than it had been.
Soon, it would have enough to eat
to fly
in the trees' tops.
Soon, oxygen would be its main meal.

"She's crownin' when she finds the ridge's top,"
Jake's voice edged its way through the dark.
"Feel the hairs bend on your arms, Willy?
That's not fear. She's sucking the air.
She's comin'." The earth vibrated under their palms.

Above the ridge,
billows of smoke brushed with red
quivered intensely until the sky flamed.
The ground continued to shake.

But it was the roar like a million bats
that brought Jake and Willy full alert.

No longer earth-bound,
the fire flew past the ridge's peak
then continued its fall toward the valley.

"No time," Jake kneeled into the dirt,
hands scooping whatever lay in his way.
"Dig. For your face,"
and Willy followed Jake's lead.

Neither had noticed night's end.
In the daylight bright red,
neither saw the other.
The world for that second
was what they flung with their hands.

The heat was on them solid
when the fire was halfway down the hill,
so as they buried their faces
into the fresh loam smell,
they had to have known.

They had to have known
as the leaves and twigs and loosened earth
were sucked into the wind
that the fire would have its way
with what it found.

Even before their lungs
fully felt the searing breath,
the first flames had passed,
jumping up the next slope,
searching for the next crest.
The following flowing flames gleaned and gathered
what was left on the tips of the trees.
The cleaned earth trembled.

Finally, the valley was closed off
from the fire
by ridge after ridge.
The light flickered out.
Silence ebbed back down the ridges
and seeped into the quickly dug holes.
The land lay charred, motionless.
Jake and Willy, arms encircling their heads,
wedged there
seeming to wait,
seeming to be.

—William T. Sweet

Autumn Drunk

But, no, not but, and, the right conjunction, and,
yes, and, it fits, starved luxury, mango time, and
the stubborn heart aches, gray trees turn green,
and we are drenched by summer rain, and blame
the gold silk those courtiers wore in ancient China,
Marco Polo mixing with the common folk, and
always looking for the just right woman, green
eyes, jewels luscious like frosted oranges, and
no wonder he stayed for seventeen years, and
got back in time to be on the losing side in war,
but the emperor was generous, set him free, and
he let his servants carry him miles through marsh
and desert, slowly past farms and rivers, boats
adrift in the free nights, and no one ever would
think someday it would be so like this, and so
overjoyed as Li Po drinking the last wine, and
the season becoming one bird singing, drunk
on the tangles of infinite questions.

—John Garmon

Youth and Its Discontents

There was a time when I was glad to know
all the roads that led away from where I lived,
or I should say I thought I knew, but all I could see
were the places where these roads began and where
they vanished as they got to the top of the horizon.
I lived in a place that was cold in the winter
and very hot and dusty during the summer.
It had its clouds and stars and its own phrasing
of what the locals called ineffable, its curriculum,
its calculus, and of course its stories, all a few words,
but mostly true. One of the oldest houses was haunted
or so the locals claimed, and the town languished
between the clear-cut ground and the dying forest.
There was a muddy fork of road in the spring
and it could have carried me away for good
if I had known which path to take, and a ditch
ran next to the wider part of an open space
climbing to a ridge that led to switchbacks
where Douglas fir held the side of a mountain
in place with bitter green strength. I didn't climb
that deadfall invitation to danger, but I wanted to.
I felt, if I could get up on top someday, I'd shout
until I was hoarse that people should wake up
and escape before the final orgasm took us down.

—John Garmon

Mother Weather

My mother threw me into thunderstorms.
When dust clouds rolled down from the north
She sent me outside to play.

She recognized how beautiful it is
Being in the center of turbulence,
Tornado warnings boiling overhead.

I often ran away with tumbleweeds
Until they stacked with their sisters
Impaled on barbed wire fences.

A thirst in my blood for storms
Led me to see the owl and hawk
As feathered weathervanes.

They sat gathered into their wings
Like ancient Chinese poets
Writing illegible lines.

My mother knew no solitude
Could ever match the lonely sound
of shingles holding in high wind.

She taught me storms are innocent
Of treachery. One summer night
We stood at our fence and watched

As the neighbors' barn rose up
And flew toward the clouds
Like an albatross in lunar seas.

Years later my mother died
And I was glad to hear
Big hail falling hard outside.

—John Garmon

By The Bay

The man on the boardwalk where it turns into a dock
makes eye contact by mistake and seems embarrassed
but he covers by looking stern. He is fishing this morning
and I am not supposed to be here. His floppy hat presses
flat against an ancient forehead wrinkled by too much sun.
He is browner than a mountain lion, and I can see his face
with its deep lines that once must have been beautiful
to a lover who was eager to feel his body, his kisses,
his arms encircling. This morning he is fathering me
and not realizing the inexplicable passions I'm feeling.
I know I shouldn't stand here looking at him, waiting
to watch as he throws the line out again, as it cracks
against the glassy surface of the bay, this morning
before the heat radiates and hurts my eyes. I wear
my white windbreaker and note his yellow raincoat
which must be too warm for this gathering day. He
finally squarely meets my eyes, commanding attention,
as if I must follow his unspoken resolution that I be gone,
move, take myself out of his autumn space. I acquiesce
and make my way down the boardwalk toward town.
I think he is not fishing, not really expecting a catch,
only here to watch the time gain momentum, the day
wearing forward as the water begins to ripple slightly
as a first breeze blows in from the mouth of the bay.
I know from time past he will be here all day.

—John Garmon

No Longer Worthy

I can't tell why today I feel no longer worthy.
These pines this morning wear a different glow,
yet I feel apart from this fresher green
on boughs of rain-rinsed needles

forgetful of their fallen brothers, who
no longer worthy of praise, still serve,
still pad each footfall, still feed each root,
still shelter the rotting womb of toadstools,

yield incense under pressure. This gentle
lift of new shoots and cleansing fragrance
rising from the path in pre-dawn mist say:
Offer yourself to wind and sun for nothing.

—William Kester

In the Rough

It might have been trod on by deer hooves,
kicked aside from the pebble path,
fractured—its full length split open
like flayed fingers of a human hand,
flattened sinews drenched with dew.

Its skin, pale green from lichen,
once tough as elephant hide, now
crumbles at the slightest touch. A hint
of tannic acid ascends like perfume
among darker flavors deep down in.

One finger grew gnarled around its neighbor
while the gaping socket of another testifies
to losses even before the fall. Shaped by time
and elements, true to its deep-soaked oak roots,
it grew tough-grained against the odds.

Whatever brought it down—the wind,
old age, disease or hard living—
could not hide the traces of a life
lived out in four directions. It asks no pity.

—William Kester

We Were Out of Town

We were out of town when spring came. Returning,
we found flowering plums, birch in green lace,
northbound clouds of small birds winging blue space
so high above melting snowbanks, yearning
toward home almost too warm for spring. Ablaze
with this sudden seasonal change, in dreams
of maples the rich golds of autumn, I seem
to trample dry reeds in wet marshes, or gaze
out on a silver husky hunched alone
beside a strap of broken harness, hear
his low moan as breaking ice cracks sharp, clear,
knowing he knows his small patch drifts and groans
  over deep currents, as his ice raft swirls
  ever out on a cold dark watery world.

—William Kester

Winter Meditation

Whispering wings. The hurrying man stops,
regards pine and eucalyptus that lean
against winter grey at this verge of copse
and open field, watches blackbirds stream,
vanish in black holes: green needle galaxies
of one rainwashed Monterey. Branches dance
in tango rhythms, witness to frenzies
of birds feasting on honeyed pine candles.

His heart urges rhythms of ritual drums,
but bittersweet eucalyptus musk clings
like dread of dark waters. Shifting his gaze,
he sidesteps a shadow's edge, keeps in sun,
haunted by after-image beating wings,
awaits the soul these birds will bear away.

—William Kester

Uncut Stone

If there is a man in a block of marble,
Then there is a quilt in a ball of yarn.

If there is a ship in the trees of the forest,
Then there is a loaf of bread
In the unplowed fields,

And if a serving of jam lies in these bushes
Just springing up out of the snow,

There is a cat's cradle in the tangled ball of string
Under the bed, and a kite in the pile
Of discarded wrapping paper.

In the sky there is a flock of birds
Who were simply born there. Everything else
Is made from something else.

When we open the cage, a bird comes out
And fills the room with feathers.

When we open the gates at the hatchery,
Rainbow trout, most of whose bones
Are no bigger than a cat's whisker,
With keen eyes and thrashing,
Swim desperately toward the lakes of the world.

—Ray Hadley

Hummingbirds

Because hummingbirds
Don't weigh anything,
And because they
Follow the course
Of blooming flowers,
They can go anywhere,
Even to South America,
On the energy of pollen.

I've extricated them
From screen doors
Pushing their beaks
Back through the mesh,
Their wings a
Flurry in my hands.

They appear out of
Nowhere, smaller
Than the bones in my wrist,
Hovering in front
Of morning glories.

They are so small,
I've mistaken them
For honey bees,
Their flight so impossible,
I'd bet against them.

I never see them at rest.
When I look in my bird book,
I learn that some live
In the tropical foothills
Beneath a volcano in Mexico.

I can't imagine the speed
Of their beating hearts, their wings,
Or how rapidly they breathe.

I've seen them wrapped
In silk pouches
On necklaces,
Good luck
For those who believe
In magic.

I've seen their eyes,
Almost empty,
As if they knew
Just how easy it would be
For them
To enter heaven.

—Ray Hadley

Wednesday Night Waltz

It was such a surprise when you threw the violin
into the fire and then the guitar, broken
beyond repair.

The strings curled and sparked, the rare woods glowed
and fell in on themselves and made no music
above the crackling of the flames.

Then, the two of you, began to play a waltz
on a violin and a guitar made out of air
so we would remember the duets
you played in the parlor

Everyone began to hum a different waltz.

Someone sang the Wednesday Night Waltz,
someone sang the Waltz du Dixie so quietly
that everyone could hear only his or her own song,
and I heard you sing distinctly and softly in French,
The Waltz That Carried Me to My Grave.

I still have that old record
you gave me by Joseph Falcon,
and only recently have I begun
to memorize the words:

"Dan la terre, c'est par toujours
 jolie fille, chere"

It was one of those fires that burn all night.
The next morning the coffee was still hot—
a caffeinated mud that tasted like gasoline,
but, when we made breakfast
we only had to blow lightly
on the coals to rekindle the fire.

—Ray Hadley

Standing In Hybrid Bermuda

An ornamental deer of woven vine
and fiber stands
silent and stares
at its living counterpart

grazing on the cultured lawn.
If this fabricated creature
could move, it would,
sensing through anchored feet

a rush of water
toward subterranean sprinkler
heads, ready to burst
with an almost erotic

release, from the grass
along the eroded edge
between civilization and the wild
propensity of nature.

—Michael Kiriluk

The City, Almost as Innocent as I

1.
I remember
 falling rain, walking streets of canvas
 awnings, water, pungent
 with gravity, dripping
 from scalloped edges, feeble
 protection for tables
 of used paperback books, their pages
 fluttering in the gusty wind.
 A young man in wool
 jacket and work boots, oiled
 to a mahogany luster, stops,
 sets down his lunch pail,
 opens a slim volume of Neruda's verse.
 In the street, a smoking moped
 buzzes by, the rider trailing
 the tails of his yellow slicker,
 like the tattered wings
of student anarchy.

2.
I remember
 the anonymity of night windows
 along quiet streets
 of California bungalows,
 their shingled sides glistening
 from a thick soaking
 by winter's first real storm.
 Front porch communists have gathered
 their collective dreams
 of revolution and moved inside,

seeking the warmth
of wainscoted rooms.
Again I would turn down
a cracked concrete
walk, lined with moss,
damp with the possibilities
of small adventures,
past old houses of old scholars
that lead to a seclusion
of backyard rentals, cottages
with leaky faucets, sloping floors
and art students, newly arrived
from distant valley towns,
longing to acquire
inspiration, validation, true love.

—Michael Kiriluk

A Tip of the Scales

He stumbled, staggered
on an uneven rock
that tipped, that
spilled him forward,

like an unsteady
drunk, or a clumsy
old man, paltry
in step, not watching

his inert feet, equilibrium
as faded as
his youth.
Two men, more
than a generation younger, move
in startled haste
toward his sprawled figure,
their concern loud

in voice and manner.
The pain of his grated flesh, blood
starting to ooze
from arm and leg, not as sharp,

not as deep as the realization
of how feeble
he appears
in their apprehensive eyes.

—Michael Kiriluk

To the Ground and its Generous Giving

Everywhere, the aroma of God begins to arrive.
—Jalaludin Rumi

The first warm day, not yet spring,
soil swells ever so slightly.
Musk begins to rise and stretch from pockets
of long hibernation,
like a hungry bear the smell roots in the nose,
wet rot of tumbleweed,
heat of humus cooking off under the sun
like rich yeast aroma ascending from the pregnant
dome of soon-to-be bread
or the sweet chocolate waft of toll house cookie.
Pungent earth, the temptation to turn a spadeful
to reach down and bring it
to your nostril, sweet snuff of nature,
roll it between your fingers,
the pads releasing the spices of dirt.

Somewhere in the gorges of Africa
Maeve Leakey is probing a rocky drift.
Another skull appears, this one not
Lucy, not the womb from which all mankind sprung
or so we were told,
but another, an interloper.   Lucy's face
was unearthed with a snout,
large teeth, prominent cheekbones. The new skull
is christened "Flat-face man,"
small toothed, incredible, the anthropologists
struggle for explanation.
But here, in my back yard, the sand and clay
are simple, diverse and anxious for seed,
cling to whatever secrets they can.

—Bill Cowee

An Age of Separation

In the beginning you barely notice,
a shifting in forces
as mysterious as the river's shoulder
shrugging in repetition against the bank—
a few grains, then a whole slide
before the blade of dirt topples, gives
itself to the current.
You see the same detachment in her eyes,
a small increment of emptiness,
a lightness of presence
as if spirit loses the way in mist.
Soon it becomes apparent everywhere.
The cottonwood drops its limbs
in higher winds, even the rose tosses its petals
at the feet of the emperor.
We live in an age of separation.
You need to be tougher,
some, say, tougher.
A heaviness descends, internal,
pleads in an authoritative voice,
let go. . .let go

—Bill Cowee

January, Looking for Employment

To be snow, long free fall, giddy plummet
into high desert, caught
by white sage, greasewood, an occasional juniper,
suspended waiting for thaw,
held for warmer winds
or weary sun barely
able to rise above icy north facing hills.
To be snow, unpretentious,
stripped of ego,
to be only snow
for which others thirst,
to be given up in being,
short moments of reality when you are
what creation assigned for you,
to be fully your naming,
fully your identity, taut like a skin.
To go, then, as you must,
the melt fierce within you,
to earth, to disappear, humble,
last wet words left upon the ground.

—Bill Cowee

Tell Me Again of the Shade in Summer

In the end one loves one's desires,
not what is desired.
                    —Nietzsche
            Beyond Good and Evil, 175

Across the Carson River, four cottonwoods died,
bark now long ago peeled. They stand together,
white limbs splayed, starkly angular,
pale crones of MacBeth huddled around the cauldron,
or four white-maned horses of apocalypse.
It is good to look on death
in the midst of life around this river.
To know the willows
wanting to be baskets will only hold the river bank
in place at high water.
Death can be subtle as life,
and incremental.
The bones of the cottonwood, bare as fallen antlers,
are plaintive,
bleached by aquifers pilfered in the meadow.
Their marrow has hardened,
their skin smoothed by a sandy whetstone.
UP! Don't wait there.
I want you to bud out, spring
is bleating in the wind.
I've driven this road for years listening.
But the white jawbones are silent, lost
in their toothless memories,
absent of water
and the pain of it all wandering
somewhere in the hayfields.

—Bill Cowee

Guadalupe Passage

The owner of the Pinon Grocery Store in Pinon, New Mexico, asks me if I have 16-ply tires on my old Ford pickup when I inquire of the back roads to Queen, New Mexico, 100 miles to the southeast.

I tell him I have plenty of time to go slow and he asks if I have 5 hours.

I look at my watch and say, "Sure."

So then he tells me how to find my way along the state, county, BLM and Forest Service roads to the little town like his own where there's only one business, a grocery store. Then he says it might be three or four days before anyone else comes through there.

Well, my truck makes it fine, but I don't. While I'm driving over this rough route, not ever seeing another human, I can't stop thinking about the woman from Houston who killed her kids because a spirit told her she needed to kill her children because they were going to burn in hell if she didn't. Dying by their mother's own hands, the spirit says, is the kids' tickets to heaven. And I wonder if she studied in Palestine.

I watch a 10-point buck bolt from the edge of the rocky road, and I wish I could have taken the homicidal mother on a trip from Pinon to Queen before she killed her children. Maybe being out of Houston would have made a difference. Maybe her spirits would have lifted if she had gone up in the Guadalupe Mountains. Maybe she'd have had a different notion of what heaven is and the children would have been able to take their own trips over primitive roads and decide for themselves about whether or not to put 16-ply tires on their vehicles and about whether or not there really is a heaven or hell and about whether or not to drive from Pinon to Queen. Perhaps if they did decide there is a heaven they would not have wanted to go to one that looks like a Baptist summer camp outside of Houston.

—Jim Harris

Prairie Coyotes

The farmer who owns the field behind my house
has been trying to kill the coyotes that serenade me
in the dark each night with their yaps and howls.

The farmer doesn't like the coyotes killing his chickens,
so he spends some nights riding around in the back of
his truck blasting away at the hungry canines.

In Louisiana they call what he is doing "bull eyeing,"
shining lights in the eyes of the game to mesmerize
them and make them stand motionless, easy kills.

In most states it's illegal, but in New Mexico the people
of the land can take drastic measures with varmints
found cutting into profits. Often they hang their trophies

on barbed wire fences to show how civic minded they are.
But when the shooting begins, I want to run into the field
and ask the farmer if he is going to replace the coyote sounds

that I have become accustomed to. I want to know if he
kills them all if he is going to give back to me the music
they have brought to my home and my neighborhood.

The truth is, no matter how much killing is done,
the farmers and ranchers won't be able to stop
the coyotes. They're too smart for humans.

They'll be serenading their sweethearts long after
the era of the farmer. When nations have given up
competing and the last human on earth blasts off

for a safer planet, it'll be the coyotes yapping and howling
when the roar of the engines subside. We'll hear them
through the microphones we will have left on the prairies.

—Jim Harris

The Candlelight

*Oh, candle, you who take fire onto yourself to burn
out, everything exists only to perish. For this reason
alone, isn't everything infinitely beautiful?*
                                                    —Naka Taro

Whatever her eyes light on leans
Into a small ring—her pillow,
Her nightgown, a table by the door—
And brighten the entire room.

Small things of the metaphysical solid
Engage and give meaning to all existence.

Even a little resistance to death
Makes her life seem more important.

Faintly diminishing trails, her eyes
Flicker like birds crossing borders.

One last witness, she becomes
The candle that burns in prayer;
Grows calm in the light,
Stays alive by banishing the dark.

—Leonard Cirino

Another One for Jeri

The flame she candles is a small prayer,
An offering to her lover's madness.
An invocation to halt suffering.

Obscure and convoluted, her lips recite
An ancient commitment to dragons
And elves, devas and tricksters.

She is dressed in forms of light
And shadow, shades of gray.

She whispers, ever so tentative.
The wind repeats her cadences.

—Leonard Cirino

Her Dreams, like Prayers

Her dreams, like prayers,
Suddenly stop
When she hears footsteps
Leading to graves in the dark.

Waking, she turns on the light.
It spreads over her body
Like a blanket or her lover.

The glow expands as she looks
For something else in her room,
Anything that distracts her from terror.

She closes her eyes and listens
To footsteps climb the attic stairs.

A small black ghost
Kisses her forehead
Like a comforting wind
From a great distance.

—Leonard Cirino

Letter to Jeri After Waking
From an Erotic Dream

Yes, there is a rhythmic pulse between us,
And when we tryst an animalism shakes
As if we were galloping toward some other
Perfect abstraction and then the earth heaves
Into a curving whirlwind like the moon
Does as she settles on the horizon
With her flanks over the waterline
And I tremble as if a mountain
Had shrugged its raw shoulders
Reserved for those who move this way
And roll in the dust and grass.

As the poet Schnackenberg says, "it's not
Just that you make me come and come
And come again," but that each time
It's as if I test the earth with a dousing wand,
Dip down, into, and hover once more
Until it is beyond itself and springs up
The way flowers return their tongues to my stare.

—Leonard Cirino

Isis and Osiris: Remembering

She can barely recollect his face now
though they were married
thirty-two years-or was it thirty-three?—
and she's taken to widowhood
(using the old-fashioned word
only to herself),
getting over the shock
of his not untimely death
(he was a good ten years older),
but now on her hands and knees
planting a row of annuals,
she still can't help thinking
about the mystery of the man
she lived with, had two children by,
who could live and die and she not recall
one word they'd exchanged,
and the face that kept popping up
was not always his face, that is, the one
she can look at in the single photo
she keeps on the mantle—lucky thing,
or she'd lose all recollection,
and like the few others, a poor likeness,
at least she thought it was,
hut how could she be sure?
And how he'd hated his picture taken,
like a kid, left the room, disappeared
as if he believed as some tribe somewhere did
that his soul—or was it his body?—
might be stolen in the snap of the shutter,
so with only a few shots left,
she put some other face on her husband
as she had sometimes imagined

when they lay in bed trying to find
sleep or as in dreams when he appeared
a grinning perfect stranger
though she felt no strangeness,
not in the dream she must confess
she still has, and today as she places
the last fat marigold into the front yard plot,
she thinks the dream face is really his
as she puts it back together:
nose, eyes, ears, finally mouth,
and she tries to imagine those lips
opening, saying something, but she wants him
full figure, pacing the room, reciting something
important: stomach thighs, and legs;
all parts, even the one that in bedroom dark
she'd rarely seen at all, and she stands up,
walks toward the old, dark house,
remembering all these pieces of him—
whether real or dreamed—into a ghost
with eyes as blue-green as a river,
staring as curious as she is,
a ghost of what might have been,
who could explain the mystery,
not of the other side,
but of what it was like before,
who would tell her so she might believe
the story of their lives.

—Philip Miller

Snow's on the Way

They say out at the airport
it's already beginning to snow,

and now the wind comes down,
a new winter storm gathers

to hit after we're in bed,
maybe waking us in the dark

with a small hiss at the window,
shadowy by its white cover

which will lie plush at dawn
for the children to discover

as a surprise, giving them
perhaps a day off from school

from learning the real reason snow
falls at all, how weather conspires

according to perfectly ordinary
laws to create something dazzling,

"lovely" is the word a few old
people still use, as that poem

once did, that children sometimes
"overhear" and remember

without knowing why, being struck
by it again and again

like the shock of sun glittering
on white at dawn for Christmas

as it sometimes does, that a song
we all try hard to forget,

hearing it so often, dreams
and dreams about—the snow coming

by accident, of course, but still
as if by order—how could children

think otherwise? Or how can we,
the elders, not wonder, too,

why snow crystal, atom, and gene—
things we can't see with our naked eyes—

spin in our brains, rotate there
like long, lost Christmas tree ornaments,

conspire to suggest laws
dazzling and lovely as the great sparkling

flakes of white snow falling
and falling for no reason at all?

—Philip Miller

Changing Colors

The dusty paint of Sierra hills
leaves my eyes wanting.
I am used to the glut
of thick green Oregon woods.
The watercolors of moss and evergreen
that wash the rooms of my mind
are slowly being covered
with the grit of sand and sun.

But I am learning to love brown.

A fine cinnamon powder
has settled on my windchime.
I blow it into the rays of morning sun
and listen for its song
as particles drift to my hand.
My fingers explore
this keyboard of sunburnt music.

In the dust on my windowsill,
I write my name
so that I may call this place home.

—Terry Forde

Geranium Music

It's probably not good to go back.
        But I need to be near the old house again.

The sagging fence, that couldn't keep life out,
still wraps the house with weathered arms.
Here and there, through its missing teeth,
high grass pokes its head to see the world outside.
They have hung a new gate.
        Perhaps it will help.

There is a young woman on the steps.
She sweeps away geranium petals,
not knowing they are mine.
A lifetime ago I carefully tucked the tender shoots
deep in the warm earth.
        But their blossoms were short lived.

I would like to sit with her on those steps
and feel the sun warm our legs.
We would sip our coffee,
drinking in the taste of morning quiet.
I would tell her about the music of my house.
        The melody of beginnings and endings.

I would share with her the soft strum
of laughter that drifted from nursery windows,
the hum of busy lives that forgot to sing together,
the adagio dance on bedsheets that faded too soon.
And, of course, the soundless tears—
        I would tell her that's how I watered the
geraniums.

—Terry Forde

Stone Houses

These stones, stolen from the rivers,
are the bookmark of centuries.
They have slept in the footprints
of mastodons and their lichen blankets
took a hundred years to weave.
They have been caressed by ancient oak roots
and seen fish begin to walk upon the land.

Now we imprison them in mortar,
no longer bathed in the cool of glaciers.
Gone is the kiss of a salmon tail
and a bluebottle's wing on their cheek.
They have been torn from their brothers
after a million years of family.

They are locked in straight lines
with their faces in the wind,
dust covering their dreams.
But deep inside, fires still glow,
for these stones know that one day
they will be given back to the river
when we are all gone.

—Terry Forde

Night Jewelry

The day fades and darkness
drapes the night skies.
Time to open the jewel box.

First is a sliver of ivory
I pin on her black slip.
Then onto her slender body, I weave
a gown from a thousand silver chains.
It slips from a sloping shoulder,
just enough to kiss the tops of mountains,
so I fasten it with a string of pearls.
Then I gather eight gold rings
to bracelet her delicate wrist.
Now a handful of opals
I braid through her dark curls.
A tiara of swirling gems.
I hang rubies from her ears.
The rest slip from my hand,
their red fire catching in the folds of her dress.
With a shake of the midnight cloth
that lines the bottom of the box,
I sprinkle the lace of a million diamonds
on her coat.

Too quickly the party is over.
I take my night jewelry,
wrap it in the sweet breeze of early morning,
and place it on moonflower petals in the velvet box.
She will go out again tomorrow night.

—Terry Forde

Fruits of Memory: Strawberry

When I finally go to meet the Maker of All Fruits
he'll be waiting with a checklist of earthly delights
for me to leave behind in exchange for hereafter.

What about strawberries? he'll boom, and I'll confess
to recalling that once I turned June into homemade jam,
the pot ridged with ruby glue, its stained glass puree
long gone, and yes, there's a photo of my daughter
age four in her new Strawberry Shortcake sweatshirt,

and isn't that what his divine Sunset Brigade
smashed and smeared over the Wisconsin lake or outside
my Indiana window above the plum-dark clouds?
And once in Illinois a single transplant grew
by the front steps, where what I remember is the image
I'll carry to heaven: one thin extension with a pearl
reaching out to ripen and start anew.

—Joanne Lowery

Fruits of Memory: Peach

Skin and curvature pale to rose,
fuzz plus crease, scrotal shell and smooth pit.
A mother who can't believe in anything bigger
than what she holds in her hand
slices a snack, peels it smooth
for the first warm season of a child
who holds it in his fist, squeezing,
sucking the tactile mess and rubbing his hair.
Out of the high chair, a damp rag cheek to cheek,
she breathes pheromones and orchards
before setting the peach down,
his golden barefoot perfection.

—Joanne Lowery

Fruits of Memory: Apricot

The first autumn of her life, her father and I
took her north into Wisconsin's burning,
bundled her into a forest green jacket
with bright orange lining, matching orange hat
in the crisp woods, leaves falling all around
for her delight and edification.
Princess Cold Cheeks, I called her,
kissing the twin apricots' velvety skin,
tawniness ruddied in the cold air.
Like some import from China
she was my body's exotic fruit
cultivated far beyond imagination.
First one side then the other
I kissed next to her toothy smile
where she glowed the color of dawn,
my daughter beautiful as a memory
long after the woods became bare.

—Joanne Lowery

Fruits of Memory: Apple

Like the mother who cannot name her favorite child,
I'll never say I like this fruit best.
But in the mid-Seventies when our exile South ended
and we returned to finish out our marriage
in the Midwest, my days empty, the future
a bare tree, I spent eight dollars on a bushel
of Delicious apples and put them in the front closet.

Like so much of my life, those years are blank
and inexplicable, an embarrassing waste, blurred
and barely salvaged. Within a dozen years
someone would bring one and leave it on my desk.
But until then, I nibbled away at my hidden bushel.
When I went to grab a coat their perfume
said: you have come to the right place
and what Eve loved, you can too.

—Joanne Lowery

Queen of the Nile Dreams

She supposes herself—At Times,
And most often—
The Queen of England or Asia,
Yet she remains in Africa—
In Nubia, to be exact—or Nairobi—
Her homeland,
First Love—Lost—
Lasting and True reflection.

Those Other Places.
Those Other personages—
She Attends.
She Pretends.

She shouts to herself in private wonder—
Amazement:

Authenticity, Authenticity.

She Longs and Longs:
Reality Reclaimed—She Quietly Smiles.
Reality Restored—She Darkly Sparkles.

She hugs herself but whimpers
Unevenly

She Revels. She Smiles. She Revels.
And She Revels Some More.
And Often—

She Promises Herself—

She Supposes Herself
As She Waits and Wants
To Be—

More than The Face,
More than The Sculpture—

More than The Memory
She Revels,
Supposes
Herself
To Be.

—Stephen Caldwell Wright

Ages of Hearts

When Man from man, his wayward mind does turn,
He fancies himself beyond vain glory.
His reluctance continues; his heart burns,
Scorches his soul, sprouts mountainous worry.

He craves innocence, sure stability
To be his friend, to confront his desires.
His urgent brain seeks, propels piety;
Inward screams of his soul quiet no fires.

Such is the world, the hero, he proclaims,
Setting himself apart, in preserving
His route to all things other than disdain,
As if Demise would be deserving.

Sheer Agony Shrouds Gallant, Smiling Face—
Tempting, Fiery, Lovely, in Lusting Grace.

—Stephen Caldwell Wright

Intellectual Scrummage

You bring to me unfailing arguments,
The likes of which I choose not to forget,
The power of which does not soon relent.
You bring language of soul without regret . . .

Scrawl waking words from caverns of your mind;
Set yourself for the roaring volleys too,
Calm nervous anger to a cautious kind;
Wage not your wars unto a Waterloo.

I want you to instill notions as fact,
A verbal advance without surrender—
The bare words heavily breathing intact,
Singing loose any abuse remembered . . .

A fleeting scar scribbled across thin air,
Cutting swiftly as if love was not there.

—Stephen Caldwell Wright

Woman Making Ovals

The ovals stretch across the lined sheet
of paper like eggs standing on end,

the dot on each the eye it sees with,
wordless whispering between neighbors,

the dance of the sugar plum zeros,
taking her secret to the edge of the page

and then starting over, always starting
over, ovals over and over and over.

—Chip Dameron

Inland Sea

After words
disappear

gray salt soup
thickens

birds and fish
go too

rowing alone
in circles

at the edge
of sound.

—Chip Dameron

Engine of Muscle

Serve off the sun
and come in,

geared for what
comes back quick,

the air all angles
and the heart

efficient as a
curt backhand

that clips the line
and ends game

and set and match,
such sweat so sweet.

—Chip Dameron

Snapshot

I guess the fellow
in the photo
doesn't need to hear
where he's gone to,
what he's missed—

he's cold but satisfied,
arm in arm
with friends now dead
or disappeared,

the day's march
against the war
about to begin,

taking him
down a long trail
that's reached this house
and this image
in my hands.

—Chip Dameron

Tattoo of a Cobra

on his leg a tattoo of a boy and girl in paradise
on his leg a tattoo of a cobra
on his leg an Indian headdress tattoo
a war bonnet skin painting
on his leg a spider a carousel horse tattoo

on his arm his father's watch
the watch of an electrician a Knight of Columbus
on his chest I don't know
I've run out of things for his chest
he's lying on a carpet and on his chest
he's balancing an empty milk carton

in his heart the girl in paradise
shouting get down from there
in his heart a winding hilly road
in his memory a houseboat on a river
and from inside the houseboat piano music

in his house a sewing machine
in his wallet an Indian head nickel
in his book of dreams a waterfall
beneath the waterfall he hears his father's
voice but can't make out what
his father is saying or to whom his
father is speaking

—Pete Mladinic

Javelina

He told me Steve Reeves
the first Hercules of cinema
the first gladiator had died.
He told me he rented a two bedroom condo
at Point Pleasant for a thousand dollars
for the last week of July.
I asked about his mother's health.
I told him I would be there
before he left for Point Pleasant.
He told me about work, how they'd
planned to make the work week
three thirteen hour days
in place of five eight hour days.
We spoke of his son's band,
industrial music played at concerts
in Milwaukee, Phillie, and St. Louis.
He said they had a foldout couch.
I said we'd find a hotel or a bed
and breakfast plus a rental car.
I forgot to tell him that one
week before, in the desert
near a mountain named Agua Fria,
a Saturday morning, a javelina
was running toward me
and Glen, from Saskatoon,
and that the javelina made
a wide arc around us
amid the sage, mesquite,
and prickly pear that blossomed
on that desert floor.

—Pete Mladinic

Seeing the Dead from a Distance

a field where helicopters would land
and from which they would rise,
a field in the corner of a rice paddy
and beside the field two streets,
an intersection. I sat in the back of a truck
and I could see them, untidy rows
which years ago I described as heaps
of laundry. This was after the first night
of Tet. It was morning and light.
We were going from the city to our barracks
on the other side of the bridge
that connected the two parts of the city.
What about the dead? I saw them
only a moment. I didn't see them
really, didn't ask the driver to stop,
didn't walk up and look into eyes
of one of the dead. Yet they
were there and I was in the truck
with others. We were wearing boots
and green fatigues. I didn't see
if the dead were wearing watches
or necklaces, or where they'd been hit.
That happened in the dark. They
were out in the rice paddy, where they died.
This is safe speculation. They died
while I stood on the roof of an admiral's
house. An admiral would come out
smoking a cigar on the roof of memory
years after that night, as one did
the night before the truck collected us
and we rode, no one saying a word.

—Pete Mladinic

Summer Night at Heron Lake

Crawdads in a net
gnats in the air mud on the ground
shoe soles and boot soles caked with mud
in the morning after a night of rain
tonight
three mud children a girl and two boys
taking crawdads in their hands and throwing
the crawdads into a fire
a crawdad covered in ashes crawling
Addy the blonde mud girl
holding one for the first time in her eight
year old hand
Addy standing above the fire
the ground dry the mud gone
from the soles of our boots
Addy with no mother Addy with her father
on a hill above the silver lake
her father in a chair a can of Tecate
in hand talking with other men and women
about sailing
the five month old Zeus
his leash tethered to a tree
sniffing the damp ground
the net for crawdads a round meshed
cannister on ground near the fire pit
the moon half visible through clouds
two kerosene lanterns one on a table one in a tree
the crawdads crawl in ashes
Addy with a thin tree branch moves one into the flames

—Pete Mladinic

Elephant Butte Lake

I wait out high-pitched boat engines
finding their secluded bays, ruptured
igneous islands, winded channels,
open waters, their captains raising
another beer to celebrate small
arrivals, the joy of distance,
the loss of shore.
I wait to hear the wakes
they abandon, the ankle-high
waves lapping the sand. They can't go
far enough away even as their hulls'
horizons diminish to a fidgeting point.
I hear from beach towels,
two teenagers compare their faulty
geometries, how the theorems of proportion
always end with the same unequal
propositions. What length to trim their purple-
dyed hair, who will take care of that last
faded rooted inch?
They have come to dislike us,
both the many and the few,
which leaves even fewer to remind us
of summer: the immense acres of light
that freckle the distant volcanic slopes,
the ragged edges of singular clouds pedestaled
on their shadows, the seagulls that fly
over desert trailing wakes of heat,
and, perhaps once or twice, how we turn
to each other to hear what's unspoken.

—Walter Bargen

Cancelled Flight

Gripped around his waist, clutched against
her body, he arches his small back to throw
himself into space, a highdiver of frustration
bypassing the wading pool for a belly flop
in the still water of waiting. She struggles
to cinch him tight to her, his legs kicking
above the polished floor as he drowns
in the rising level of his caterwauling.
Her voice pressurized, sinks
into lower octaves, a wide wake
of scorched syllables. Her hands rivet
his squirming ankles. He's already gone
under a fourth time. Her hand raises,
but then she stops, she can save herself.
Flushed crimson when he's set down,
he turns to bury his face in the chair.
Holding to the arm rests, he continues
to kick, having lost all surfaces
in the terminal crowded with connections.
He begins to run under water.

—Walter Bargen

Parental Advice

A set of plans,
we can't get around that.
It doesn't mean that we follow
the straight-and-narrow,
that we plan anything at all,
or that we fall into someone else's plan,
maybe not meant for us,
or meant for us and we let it happen.
We perceive a plan in order to device
another plan. Often we stumble
between plans and act as if we don't care.
Rarely is not caring the case.
In ancient Antioch the citizens belonged
to both synagogue and church,
hedging their bets that the Romans
wouldn't slay both on the same day.
They coughed dust either way,
still a plan.

*

Morning traffic on eight lanes of 270
looping Saint Louis has stopped.
Even at this early hour.
Even leaving earlier than needed.
A mother turns to her son,
half asleep in the seat next to her,
his head leaning against
the closed window, rocking slightly
with each lurch forward.
North bound between Olive and Page,
trucks and cars another layer

of concrete. Who could conceive
of so much potential, idling beyond
possibility. What's the hold up,
the obstruction, construction,
sleeping-at-the-wheel destruction,
engine fire, fatalities? They will never know.
Both hands gripping the steering wheel,
she turns to her half-awake son,
"This is another reason. If you were married,
you'd be taking a cab."

—Walter Bargen

The Unmaking of Forever

as we think about how these hours last
so slightly longer than the initials
which the rain so evenly carves
into concrete as it falls,
you may wonder at the powerlessness
of ever believing that something about us
is forever
illusion welded to the wind.

yet I will tell you that the stars contain
hieroglyphics which, although I can't translate,
I can admire for what   I choose
for them to read,
and I can tell you that the power of the rain rests
not in what it tries to inscribe
but in the unmaking of itself
from brown grass into green.

—Craig Hadden

Hand Writing

can you see?
the hand
      writing
these letters
      without ayes
without nays
just a simple blind
negation
of a
      motion
braided to this page
where
each letter, a strand
of me
      white fingers
tapping cane-like on the keys
right this instant
the hand
      writing
          sea
you
   can

—Craig Hadden

Ice Dam

bare-handed despite the winter cold
I ascend roof high to assault
the ice dam on the north side of my house.
fingers open and close upon the handle
of the hatchet seeking
a grip my swiftly numbing hand might feel,
feet perched and balanced between
this fear of falling and the embrace of the moment.
my arm rises higher than the arc of winter sun,
elbow cocked, teeth clenched, eyes
aimed at the secret heart of this glacier,
this silver gray indolence of ice
that I hope to crack with the first blow.
but the blade strike sends only small slivers of ice
flying, some glancing off my cheeks
like angry birds protecting some December's nest,
leaving tears of water to drip from my skin.
yet undeterred, my arm swoops hatchet heavy.
another blow becomes another, another, an
other blow until my wrist tires and twists
allowing my fingers to smash into the now jagged ice.
they are so numb that I cannot feel the wound, but I watch
tiny drops of red swell from this nick
chirping to be fed by my attention.
so carefully I descend, imagining
yet another scar to mark the migration of one more winter,
of one more ice dam, which now must wait
for a sun to climb just high enough
to make it slide all
by itself.

—Craig Hadden

Labels

our labels become a compass
guiding the course of our relationships,
transfixing our gaze
on the needle of security
of knowing who we always should be.

our labels straighten all lines
keeping us safely behind the bars,
pretending to have discovered the shortest distance
between you and me
by naming what we are.

our labels are not the blackness
navigating among the pinpoints of starlight
charting so neatly what has never been
until our compass leads us to true North,
lost forever in a blizzard of what could never be.

—Craig Hadden

Alignment

Excuse my abrupt exit:
I have an appointment
with my cosmic chiropractress.
Yes, I've been metaphysically
out of line again:
questioning the gods
in front of witnesses,
taking a fatalistic attitude
toward blood in my stool.

Whenever
existential angst overtakes me
I call my manipulator
and have my outlook
popped back into place.
She cracks my brain
like knuckles,
gets my ventricular fluid
flowing like current.

The snap of cranial cartilage
cures my Schopenhaurean slump,
turns attention away from
Big Questions
toward food and sex.
In short it makes me
normal, average.

But lately
she's taken to adjusting me
only with a hammer:
says she won't lay hands on
someone without a spine.

—Paul Dilsaver

Corwin Psychiatric Ward

Despite the green drapes,
tan walls,
and brown tile,
the room reeks of whiteness.

And the staff,
dressed in street clothes
as part of the hospital's
"new policy,"
radiates so whitely
that you crave
a pair of those plastic shades
the eye doctor gives
after dilating pupils.

White is the word
of this world,
and white is how
they'll drain your mind
if they can.

So you
lie in your white room
burning eyes
on white ceiling,
listening to
white vibrations,
spine freezing
on white sheets,
while all the time
your hue-thirsty mind,
dwelling on your
nurse-possessed razor
and itchy wrist,
spawns an unmistakable
lust for red.

—Paul Dilsaver

Disconnected

I've moved on, old friend,
out past the need for
plumbing and fences,
beyond the necessity
of phone lines and electricity.

You could reach me by post
if I'd only crawl to town
and collect my mail.
But who would I hear from?
The woman who turned
my heart to five pounds of scab?

No, civilization's grown too uncivil.
I need sunshine, not communication.
So let the carcinogenic rays
rot this pumpkin on my neck
and all the dead dreams inside it.
These rattlers and porcupines
can remind me
of the people I knew when
I get sentimental.

You'll find me
when you need me.
Follow the buzzards
toward the jagged mountains
and setting sun

—Paul Dilsaver

Garden Lie

Lies slither from their holes
and wrap round my feet,
spiral up my legs
toward my scrotum hanging
like an apple.

Snakes have come
to collect the debt
owed them from Eden.
Their diamond heads
split like books down the middle,
fangs sharp and dripping.

I open my mouth to scream.
Only my forked tongue comes out.

—Paul Dilsaver

Words

The world does not need words. It articulates itself
in sunlight, leaves, and shadows. The stones on the path
are no less real for lying uncatalogued and uncounted.
The fluent leaves speak only the dialect of pure being.
The kiss is still fully itself though no words were spoken.

And one word transforms it into something less or other—
illicit, chaste, perfunctory, conjugal, covert.
Even calling it a *kiss* betrays the fluster of hands
glancing the skin or gripping a shoulder, the slow
arching of neck or knee, the silent touching of tongues.

Yet the stones remain less real to those who cannot
name them, or read the mute syllables graven in silica.
To see a red stone is less than seeing it as jasper—
metamorphic quartz, cousin to the flint the Kiowa
carved as arrowheads. To name is to know and remember.

The sunlight needs no praise piercing the rainclouds,
painting the rocks and leaves with light, then dissolving
each lucent droplet back into the clouds that engendered it.
The daylight needs no praise, and so we praise it always—
greater than ourselves and all the airy words we summon.

—Dana Gioia

Elegy with Surrealist Proverbs as Refrain

"Poetry must lead somewhere," declared Breton.
He carried a rose inside his coat each day
to give a beautiful stranger—"Better to die of love
than love without regret." And those who loved him
soon learned regret. "The simplest surreal act
is running through the street with a revolver
firing at random." Old and famous, he seemed *démodé*.
There is always a skeleton on the buffet.

Wounded Apollinaire wore a small steel plate
inserted in his skull. "I so loved art," he smiled,
"I joined the artillery." His friends were asked to wait
while his widow laid a crucifix across his chest.
Picasso hated death. The funeral left him so distressed
he painted a self-portrait. "It's always other people,"
remarked Duchamp, "who do the dying."
I came. I sat down. I went away.

Dali dreamed of Hitler as a white-skinned girl—
impossibly pale, luminous and lifeless as the moon.
Wealthy Roussel taught his poodle to smoke a pipe.
"When I write, I am surrounded by radiance.
My glory is like a great bomb waiting to explode."
When his valet refused to slash his wrists,
the bankrupt writer took an overdose of pills.
There is always a skeleton on the buffet.

Breton considered suicide the truest art,
though life seemed hardly worth the trouble to discard.
The German colonels strolled the Île de la Cité—
some to the Louvre, some to the Place Pigalle.
"The loneliness of poets has been erased," cried Éluard,
in praise of Stalin. "Burn all the books," said dying Hugo Ball.
There is always a skeleton on the buffet.
I came. I sat down. I went away.

—Dana Gioia

The Lost Garden

If ever we see those gardens again,
The summer will be gone—at least our summer.
Some other mockingbird will concertize
Among the mulberries, and other vines
Will climb the old brick wall to disappear.

How many footpaths crossed the old estate—
The gracious acreage of a grander age—
So many trees to kiss or argue under,
And greenery enough for any mood.
What pleasure to be sad in such surroundings.

At least in retrospect. For even sorrow
Seems bearable when studied at a distance,
And if we speak of private suffering,
The pain becomes part of a well-turned tale
Describing someone else who shares our name.

Still, thinking of you, I sometimes play a game.
What if we had walked a different path one day,
Would some small incident have nudged us elsewhere
The way a pebble tossed into a brook
Might change the course a hundred miles downstream?

The trick is making memory a blessing,
To learn by loss the cool subtraction of desire,
Of wanting nothing more than what has been,
To know the past forever lost yet seeing
Behind the wall a garden still in blossom.

—Dana Gioia

New Year's

Let other mornings honor the miraculous.
Eternity has had festivals enough.
This is the feast of our mortality,
The most mundane and human holiday.

On other days we misinterpret time,
Pretending that we live the present moment.
But can this blur, this smudgy in-between,
This tiny fissure which the future drips

Into the past, this fly-speck we call *now*
Be our true habitat? The present is
The leaky palm of water that we skim
From the swift, silent river slipping by.

The new year always brings us what we want
Simply by bringing us along—to see
A calendar with every day uncrossed,
A field of snow without a single footprint.

—Dana Gioia

It Starts With the Dining Room Table

paper like snow burning what's
left stains on the Heywood
Wakefield blonde veneer, the
shades down, the Venetian
blinds in the living room always
even. There were bars across
the windows to be sure my
sister and I wouldn't tumble
out. Later my mother leaned
against them, watching for my
yellow car then the cream
one, the black one. She'd run
down, the stair's treads were
mostly worn from, probably
stood three hours maybe calling
my house to make sure my
visit wasn't just imagined or I
wasn't taken hostage, didn't slip
in the tub. If someone dies
fast, there are things you couldn't
say but the slow dissolving,
bones emerging like a skeleton
of some boat emerging haunts.
Words freeze and the imprint of
wreckage is ghostly. Images of her
grasping hospital rails, her bones
jutting, her face already skeletal
sting like the sound of the pine
coffin lowered or leaving her under
a blue blazing sky, alone, in the dark

she began to be frightened of,
never wanting the light out. Or to
have a night without someone
beside her. I think of Indians
who didn't leave corpses in the
earth but raised them into branches.
Think of my mother lifted toward the light
in her green sweater, not under the
wooden ceiling but close to what was
alive and growing, having the
sky hold her

—Lyn Lifshin

Kiss, Baby, the New Film

a much more rare obsession than mine, tho
in some ways, not that different. The woman
in love with what's dead, what's given up
on breathing, caring, could be me knocking
my knuckles raw on your metal door while
you gulp another beer, put your head down
on the table. With you, it often was like
singing to someone in a casket the lid was
already down on, still expecting something.
She buried animals in the woods, didn't mind
touching them. Though I made our nights into
something more, I could have been coiled
close to a corpse. No, that part is a lie. Your
body was still warm. It was everything inside
where your heart must have been that was
rigid, ice. The woman in the film went to work,
an embalming assistant. Isn't that what I'm
doing? Keeping you with words? Embracing
you on the sheet of this paper, a tentative
kiss on cold lips, the cuddling of cadavers?
In the film, the woman says loving the dead is
"like looking into the sun without going blind,
is like diving into a lake, sudden cold, then
silence." She says it was addictive. I know about
the cold and quiet afterward, how you were a
drug. If she was spellbound by the dead, who
would say I wasn't, trying to revive, resuscitate
someone not alive who couldn't feel or care
with only the shell of the body. Here, where no
body can see, I could be licking your dead body
driving thru a car wash. I could be whispering
to the man across the aisles, "bodies are addictive."
Our word for the loved and the dead are the same,
the beloved, and once you've had either while you
have them, you don't need any other living people
in your life

—Lyn Lifshin

139

He Said It Was a Saturday Morning

I was just off from work.
nothing on tv and I'm
in my haying underwear,
an old ragged sweatshirt.
I'm smoking up a storm,
had 2 or 3 beers, feel
relaxed. Then there's a
knock, knock and I go and
it's 2 Jehovah witnesses, a
woman and a man and
they say you want to let us
come in, talk of religion.
I'm telling you my place is
sparse. I get out a beach
chair, a pillow. By the time
I'm on my 5th Schlitz, I was
real talkative, especially by
the 6th. It's 8 o'clock. I'm
rambling, "let me ask you
this, let me ask you this,"
like I'm doing a talk show.
Finally by 9 they said, in a
daze, "can we go?" and
"You don't want us to come
back do you?" and I said,
yeah, I don't think so

—Lyn Lifshin

The Day the Dogwood Bloomed

Surely, you remember the last of the frost
upon your bedroom window, above the sill

laden with glass bottles and dried corsages
from homecomings and spring proms.

You were certain those moments of adolescence
would forever be etched into the frozen glass,

or in the final vestige of winter's struggle with spring,
like a downpour lingering deep into the night.

What was left for you in this resignation,
in the fingerprints or the hollow breath

of shadows streaked upon the pane?
Where in your assurance did you bleed?

Like the purity of dogwood unfolding,
despite great objections from the cold,

you opened, a pink flushed petal
and gave what fragrance you had away.

—Pam Alvey

Moonstones and Sego Lilies

When dusk breathes the last of its light
I wander where tongue-less bells toll,
where no one else can see
the glen where we stand,
a weald only you know.

In that twilight I am the seer,
the sego lily watching for rain,
knowing that as it descends,
the drops will nourish and sustain,
give lifeblood to all who seek it.

Daybreak comes and all this darkness
is lost inside the shadows of our forbearers,
my dreams of you linger like prophecy
that will obtain a place for you
among the moonstones.

—Pam Alvey

From Yolk and Sand

Steller's jay and mountain chickadee fly
past the kitchen window, hold
sprigs of green in their beaks,
as if a ransom paid to a kingfisher
or a white-crowned sparrow.

They will not be detained by
the current of a winter May
or the rain that pelts down upon them,
as the course of storm exhales
across the valley floor.

They do not adhere
to what might be, but grasp
that which cannot be held,
the moment sand turns to pearl
or yolk becomes a beating heart.

—Pam Alvey

The Lessons of March

There is resignation in broken branches
that lay behind the winter barn,

the smell of hay and tack, faded
as rotting wood, left layered piece by piece.

The degrees of cold dampen the need
for further use in this season.

There, in the ray of filtered light
a barren womb has cried,

though the tears shed were not of salt, they were
drenched in the pain in which they bled,

and the branches which fell in high wind, remain
scattered on ground that no longer holds a place for them.

—Pam Alvey

Humans

humans humans humans
eco centric
dependent
unable able
all sublimation a way to creation
of more humans than can be sustained
techno-made noble savage limp wimp
chest beaters scratchers covers up sublimation
a way to creation
humans humans humans

in our offices we are gathered
to make our policies true
disabled by our agreements
i am not speaking to you
i do not see you
i do not feel you
i see you
i feel you
you

in our cars we are traveling
along the asphalt path
following one another
into cities and gathering places

we must make we must make
we must make we must make

coming home one evening
i stopped beside the asphalt path
to wonder the end of the day
i saw the sun drop like a stone
and i wept because the day turned to darkness
so little time to make
so little time to make

we are the only ones
that reckon dying
such finite beasts
we are lap up the sun
swallow pieces of infinity
as if famine rages our bodies
and consumes our meager meal of time

disparity is among us
we do despair
when we are joined together
only then or in pain does
the beast experience self
contracting the pleasure of being
we are nearly free from logic
we are making
we are making
to make is to believe
is to be

one day while following the asphalt path
i saw that we are travelers
restless disguisers of our nature

yeah i'm gunna find what's good
about the moral animal
the one that made words into history
built the notion of compassion
desire
love
recognized the naked ape.

we roll our bellies to the sun
say we had enough
will our enemy decline the slaughter?

our complicated nests include
the music of each other

mostly we are in love
with our selves
our kind our tribe
we look to each other
group-think the tribe
survive the progress

the politics of envy
holding each other down
holding each other might
explode the political myths
unearth the dangerous weapons
of the beasts of prey

logic, the dangerous weapon
of the moral animal
the gestures of submission
the psycho-physiological mechanism
of the submissive attitude
obstruction in the central nervous system
of the aggressor that is:

the beast without pace
the beast without pace
the beast without pace
the beast without pace

Notes:
"The wolf has enlightened me: not so that your enemy may
strike you again do you turn the other cheek toward him, but
to make him unable to do it.

When, in the course of its evolution, a species of animals
develops a weapon which may destroy a fellow-member at
one blow, then, in order to survive, it must develop, along
with the weapon, a social inhibition to prevent a usage which
could endanger the existence of the species." (Konrad Lorenz,
King Solomon's Ring)

which is easier
the making of weapons
or not using them?

why do humans have so much to say
yet rocks are silent and animals too
save a few yelps and moans

to bare the dark side
is to measure love.

i am determined to love
and be amazed that we are less violent
than we are
that we are moral animals
by choice and not compunction

we did not receive our weapons
we made them

we'll have their lives
on line
and if they confess
we Save their Deletion
the microprocession
through our forgiveness
though our biosociology
but if they do not confess
then we are bound to Delete

o moral animal you are blessed
o moral animal you must process
o moral animal you are in love

—Peter Christensen

The Professor's Song

for John Berryman

you chose to drink with us old friend
and we learned much from your oral tirades

you also chose dark water
and couldn't be reached

for you never surfaced
long enough to be touched

the uncertain night was master
where we sat concealed and alone

frightened and restless
before the storm we searched for an answer

but when there was an inkling of light
you always pulled the shades

—Richard D. Houff

My Friends!

with apologies to Emanuel Bove

they are missing in action
—meaning: from our abode
with empty pockets
and my own
in desperate need
of tithes
—preferably cash

but hell
i'd do the same thing
like being in their shoes
moving away from
me and mine

but we survive
so we're ok

—Richard D. Houff

My Mother Was a Whore

during the 50s
you had to have an image
girls & boys
were supposed to graduate
into ozzie & harriet
or june & ward
perfection

being a virgin
meant healthy marriage vows

my mother didn't quite fit into the picture
being branded a whore
was like having a death sentence
hanging over your head

she told me the whole story
on her 70th birthday

about riding horses on the farm
& the feisty arabian:

her legs spread wide apart
the painful tear in her groin
the bloodstains in her pants
losing her virginity without knowing

the old man left her
with six kids to raise & no regrets

in parting
she claimed a preference to horses over men—
they take the apples in good stride
and don't ask questions

—Richard D. Houff

I & Thou

joe is a homeless boxer
that claims he could've made it
to the top of the middleweight
    division

i've heard that same song
and dance over the years—every
punching bag has a story

my own ended with
a brain tumor removal
and a hooked scar—so much
for the fight game

it's a money angle:
for the poor; we need fatter wallets
and the rich need gladiators

and there are no bargaining chips in the game—
forget the dream
                    it's not in the cards

—Richard D. Houff

Alzheimer's Pantoum

My uncle asks, Who was that nice fellow
who drove us here?
Memory returns or it doesn't,
like using an old sewing machine.

Who drove us here?
I could thread it from memory
like using an old sewing machine.
That was your son-in-law.

I could thread it from memory, but
he doesn't remember that he doesn't remember.
That was your son-in-law.
This is the way to thread a needle.

He doesn't remember that he doesn't remember
she says, her hand on my arm.
(This is the way to thread a needle)
But he's still a sweet man,

she says, her hand on my arm.
My aunt lies with me on the hammock,
and says, but he's still a sweet man.
I recall a honey-colored suit, three buttons.

My aunt lies with me on the hammock.
On your mother's old sewing machine—
a honey-colored business suit
lined with yellow rayon.

On your mother's old sewing machine!
Hooks and eyes and a zipper,
lined in yellow rayon
and made of wool—for a 12-year-old!

Hooks and eyes and a zipper—
Brain rebels and fingers ache in memory—
a wool suit for a 12-year-old
but I never wore it.

Fingers ache in memory,
Memory returns or it doesn't,
I never wore it, and
my uncle asks, Who was that nice fellow?

—Anne Macquarie

Early Sun: Benson Lake

I want to take my friends to Benson Lake.
It will be the lame brigade, the team
of one-breasted women, women with laugh lines,
titanium knees, varicose veins, stainless steel arteries.

Those who can no longer walk forty miles
—up and down Cold Canyon, Spiller Canyon,
Virginia Canyon, Matterhorn Canyon—
will ride red mares, horses who know
these trails better than any army mule.

We'll stop at all the places
trail crews used to camp. We'll sit around
rusty stoves we might find there
and remember the way we used to watch
young men—shoulders and forearms
hard from lifting rocks and pulaskis—
watch them watch us eat Murphy's cooking:
pancakes and eggs, sausage and bacon, stew,
gritty coffee and lemonade.

And of how we went, alone, to our tent,
dreamed of young men's bodies,
and walked off the food the next day.

At the beach at Benson Lake we will agree
it's still the best place. *Ice-black lake lined with cliff*
white granite sand backed by willow (sandpiper nest)
backed by aspen, backed by lodgepole and waist-high grass.

In a basin of dark rock.
Trout in the depths
Warm sand.

We could stay here forever
—What's to go back to?—
and become a tribe of old ladies
in the wilderness, howling through August nights,
spooking campers, startling hikers,
leaving ragged footprints in the dust
and eventually, bones.

—Anne Macquarie

Note: Title and italicized material are from Gary Snyder's poem "A Walk."

Tiger Widow Villages

Where we talk after the barn door is closed, after the mare
is put away nickering for the night, her mouth in the grain.

Or the night before, tripping over the dog who sleeps in visible
across the linoleum in the kitchen, as the day was about to end
and didn't.

When we count bones, count teeth, reckon borders all over
again.
I don't know what to say to You or what You will say to me.

Silence named me like the woman compelled to put that child
in the river
in his small nest of reeds, knowing downstream was only
downstream, but away.

Living sprawled somewhere between the weeping for it and
the necessity
to go up the stairs. How is it that faith presides at this precise
juncture?

As walking away becomes the animal in the dark, feeding.
Death visits but does not stay. As falling becomes the decision
to rise.

Someone tended furnaces for a lifetime. Someone else
knew only to sing, and brightly, and not in the choir.

A child knew only happiness and another only regret. When
You ask me what I know to say about it, all I know to tell You
is that

Across the world from me there are entire villages in
Sundarbans
dedicated to those who have been taken in a glance by tigers

Who rise from the river unbidden. The shoeless children
                                                    whose fathers
are cremated there don't doubt Your mystery. An always of
                                                    arrival.

And I, feeding a horse, walking back to the house from the barn,
touch so lightly my daughter's arm as we cross the rain wet
                                                    pasture;

Leave a light burning as if when whatever it is that happens,
happens, we might be ready for it, we might love after it is done.

—Robin Elizabeth Holland

Time In Orange Or

Think about it, no, don't, know it. Wave, arrow.
It doesn't happen that way. Oh, it's all gone away,
and still is there, or wants to be there, or here, insists.
The way one thing, a noun, placed, is some thing
to you or to me. As in, her hair. Listening to that,
and going. Possessive? One frame to the next.

At each frame, something lost, or gone. Honest, believable.
Or becoming, as one thing becomes another. Witnessed. Is it
her hair fresh from the bath, that single tendril drenched,
                                             fragrant;
or the moment before it was wet? The salty scent? Was it
                                        the moment
the water entered the hair and changed it, what could not
                                        return?
Was it the changing itself? Presence, entry, permanence?

Or your grandmother's hair drenched in a storm and the hail
falling on fields, sprinkling the canteloupes like a summer
                                        delicacy
served up on a bed of ice? Or the question, orange and white
in combination, in any form? Not about the dead child's hair
                                        at all?
But your small hands braiding your grandmother's hair,
                                auburn and grey, then,
after the storm while men slowly picked up strewn sticks
                                from the yard?

As in the sunrise this morning as trumpet swans rose up
from the bland grey trees and went echoing their way
to whatever, and the salmon light sprawled out in bands
above the white reflection of stubborn morning cloud-bank
above the river. No questions. Tangles, nets of occurrence.
Somehow, wildly: mindful intent. This possible every here now.

—Robin Elizabeth Holland

Ode to the Senator Who Sent Her Children to Live with Mother in Spain for Fear the Colombian Rebels Might Kidnap Them During Her Bid for the Presidency

Until they remember your voice, quiet, timorous on the radio,
your children scurried to Spain because you were not a man
in a country whose spleen has been driven from its body,
whose only voice has tortured the walls of buildings,
the echo of boots coming for the few who choose
to make the uncertain home, how you spent the last day
with the feral press driving to people who had no radio,
no public heart for the wasted drama of the next election,
a lone vocal cord on the street lavishing condoms on men
whose backs only knew labor, not leaders like you
who blew into the silence of a nameless cocaine field,
the sour leaves would not lie down, your children pirated
away to the matriarch, how the vessels purpled in your face
when they said, *Tú eres de otro país,* that other borderless
country of Marquez where women circumnavigate
the globe of small hearts and perfume the diary of dying
with their vespered sighs, oh motherless children, she wanted
you to live without the story of kissing her blue hands.

—Shaun T. Griffin

After Neruda

My youngest pedals the dirt to Jumbo Grade.
At the cloud summit, a meadowlark
turns down the snow
on our brown mountain,
a stone come to flower.
In six short weeks, sheep will cut
the mule ears from these slopes.

All night, Neruda ebbed
at sleep. He would ease
the bedsprings and soup cans
from this mountain, pick
the bony masks of cow and coyote
and rattle them in a poem.

My boy and I wheel
the first odes to spring,
the dog chases a butterfly
shadow, the great one winging
from his window in Isla Negra—
the mollusks, the beetles
and the narwhal looking on.

—Shaun T. Griffin

The Heart Donor

I

You whisper into the forest of small hearts,
the slow unraveling of flesh to valve
with but half to own, the marriage of finite halves
in your chest. You wait for a call that will save—
the flight to surgeon who will seam skin
with the organ of another. The odds of undoing
are precise: for you to live, one must die.
Her fingerprints must find yours, the muscle jigsaw to lungs.

Your face belies the witness of uncertainty.
You are a woman at the breast of another
not far from the hands of youth,
her face a shadow of warm tones, the unspent diary
of her days. A collage of names waits for her—mother, worker,
woman who speaks with her unborn children. The chemistry
of waiting for that which is unknown,
as yet unloved, but she will wake you in the dark,
kiss the brow of your lithe frame
and answer with her life. She will seam one from two,
slip from your hands as you start to thank her.
And she will follow to old age—

II

She who receives will not know how it came.
She will not know what car you were driving,
what word you spoke before breath entered for the last time.
She will name you mother and you will unfold in her
all the wisdom of your half-life, the quizzical turntable
that found you donor, lifted from lungs that she might
always breathe your first word in thanks. There will be no
                                                    silence
to commemorate the algorithm of pulse to pain.
She will fold a letter and wish it to arrive at your door
but you will not be there. You will answer with your life—
and she who receives will dream the address of the living,
become what each could not, the singular metronome
of two hearts undone.

—Shaun T. Griffin

A Mind for Life

*The brain is prone to weave the mind from the
evidences of life, not merely the minimal contact
required to exist, but a luxuriance and excess
spilling into virtually everything we do.*
—Edward O. Wilson
*Biophilia: The Human Bond
with Other Species*

It's in everything—life,
curled to the core of each cell,
a world inherently swelled
with graceful expressions, space
and form, norms of reaction,
interactions colorfully-coded,
evolving, flowing, growing,
organically blessed, carbon-based,
nitrogen-driven codons; still, we go on
as if unseeing—oh, the acidity
of our corrosive tendencies
to tamper, dampening
the sweetly natured spirit
in this planet. A diversity
of godforms must be laughing
at our protean ambitions
and enzymatic habits of hubris.

How hypothesize socially biological
distance between a memory and a dream
scripted in DNA? In that phylogenetic
signature with syntactic pathways
lighting patterns, recurrent
neural transmissions transcend

substrates. Gray area matters,
but beyond dendrites and axons
the psyche is no accident
with immense propensity
to recognize elemental connections
apart from fears or affections
and culture's conjectural projections;
humanity historically extends
as one dimension of Earth's design
inclined with a mind to reconcile
human nature with the future of life.

—Yvette A. Schnoeker-Shorb

Sustainability of the Soul

*The historical link between work, community, and
nature, once the basis for a secure and sustainable
sense of place, has eroded. A new kind of alienation
has taken its stead.*

—Stephen R. Kellert
*The Value of Life: Biological
Diversity and Human Society*

Where is grace in estrangement? As one
of many expressions of Earth,
we have spent too much time
rattling the neural gates that divide
paradise from Eden and not enough
at synaptic junctions connecting
our impulses to affiliate
with this diverse community
to know that we are not
inclined to recombine
the elements of self
                    to matter
without relationships to others
who define us by design
in this evolving journey.
Labor intensely as we do
at the expense of the rest of creation,
we cognitively economize our fall,
gaining the freedom to return
                            to forever,
but having lost our essential place.

—Yvette A. Schnoeker-Shorb

The Evidence of Spirit

*Embodied spirituality requires an understanding that
nature is not inanimate and less than human, but animated
and more than human.*

—George Lakoff and Mark Johnson
*Philosophy in the Flesh: The Embodied
Mind and Its Challenge to Western Thought*

Here is my spirit:
hydrogen, oxygen, nitrogen,
and carbon-based, night regions
spirally bound and ringing
the center of the soul,
DNA phosphatefully linked,
rich in ribose,
but nothing sugary is coated
into the elements
crafting sweet civilization
from the culture of the Earth,
an integrity of integument,
a membrane of species,
10 million cellular expressions,
family connections—
only 1.5 million named.

Even in this postmodern game,
the brain form
contents itself with relativity,
ecologies of morals,
and textual journeys; myth
may define boundaries,
but edges depend on electrons
stitching the soul
into an evolutionary weave,
the universe animated
by that exquisite electrogenesis
where dwells the nature
of human spirit.

—Yvette A. Schnoeker-Shorb

You Who Gave Us The Sun

Leaves seek the corners
where no one steps, prowl
furtively down the edges of fences looking
for gaps they can slip through. Dead
leaves settle in the scoop of earth
at the boles of old, barren sycamores.
This is not their season.

There is no color left. Even the sun
lays itself gently upon us, no warmth,
no illumination. Why seek the tropics?
All that is heard, all that can be
heard is the distant
rumor of a beach, the soft
whisperings of water, how
its motion pushes at the meridian, pushes
hips around, and the old man
and the lean-to and the guitar
that sang to us all night long: *why not?*

But the leaves won't stop agitating.
They are worried. You who gave
us the sun are gone, and they cry
all night long, even in their deep,
narrow house, protected
by the long root-runs.
I can hear them.

—Michael Seltzer

What I Thought

We chose badly when we bought this place.
Of course it was the end of summer
and from the stoop we could sip the simmered
oolong and watch the green thin
from grasses, and the slow growth of gold.
We thought that would be enough.

We hadn't checked the floors for swelling
and no one told us there was nothing
behind the paneling, nothing that might
withstand winter, and now it's turned
cold and the anemic furnace just can't
make up the difference. The pads

of my fingers press
lightly against the storm window,
feel the frost. My hand
pulls back, leaves something behind: you

wanted to travel south for pumice
stones, to pile them against
our walls. *The rocks
will remember summer for us,* but I
said that was nonsense, let the cold
be cold, while all the time you were watching
through the window in your shift. What

steam I can generate now fogs what I see.
I thought we could insulate this place
with soft words and slender gestures. I thought
there was no need for flint, just the occasional
smile. I thought that would be enough.

—Michael Seltzer

Remember the Willows

The sun lifts over the bright edge
of the eastern hills as if rising
on its own heat, as if rotation never
really mattered, as if love is all
anyone needs to rise. The dry

grey grasses lean to the desert, turn
briefly to filaments of gold then
succumb to the light and the easy
breath of morning. Even the dog
food plant's column

of smoke, stretched thin along the roll
of the hills, disappears
in mist and morning dew. In a cold
season, this will be a warm day.
I could pull a chair near a window—

the wing-backed one, your favorite
Aunt's, worn, faded, the weave
more visible than the pattern, and take
comfort in the unknowable shapes
of warmth that pool

in my lap like a small bird
preparing for flight. I could drink
the half cup of coffee you left. Or maybe curl
in the quilt with the double wedding
ring design on your side of the bed

and read the worn paperback tucked
under your pillow. In the afternoon
I could walk: I'll take the path by the river, move
into the land,
make for the willows. Remember

the willows? That day
when the light was weak, and we
thought, maybe some air… There was nothing
between us and the blue-green of the distant trees
but the brown earth and brown

growth. You said there's water
there we don't know about; below
ground, there is mercy. I'll step
lightly, the way you do
in the morning leaving for work,

so not to disturb the tender
and timid things. And I'll wait
for the sun to find its way through
the western mountains. Then
I will hear you approach, the engine

of your car going still, your foot
in the grasses, and I'll turn
to you and feel the quail
deep within the body flush
from cover and take flight.

—Michael Seltzer

Midnight Moon

Would he understand
if tonight I pushed the bed against
the wall, beneath the window,
so I could kneel in the moonlight
as it spread silver over our sheets?

Would he understand
why I'd press my nose to the screen
inhaling completely, just
as wind lifted the embrace
of surrounding white oaks?

Would he understand
my desire, allowing the breeze
to carefully caress my face
or my hunger to hold
moist, perfumed air deep
within my lungs?

—Pat Magnuson

Dog Days

On the far side of the summer
solstice, the sky's sharpest star
rises with the sun to slow my steps, even
as the days shorten. I begin to listen for
a warning that summer grows dim.
Late, before the sky deepens
and the "dog star" struts at Orion's
heels, I wait for the crickets first notice.
Soon I will gather up my garden,
watch the squirrels clear the lawn
of acorns, search the mid-afternoon
trees for the first leaf turning.

—Pat Magnuson

Big Bang Poetry
for Deb

So matter-of-factly
you ask, "When are you going to write
one for me?"
"It's not that easy," I
say. "You have to do
something." And for barely
a breath, I imagine you swirling
around me arrayed
in some silly costume.

Do you think
we merely pluck
from some ever-expanding
word constellation?
Do you think
we order and reorder
like a preschooler's
magnetic letters on
the refrigerator door?
Do you think
we just
make this stuff up?

—Pat Magnuson

Summer Sunset on the Lake
for Robb and Mara

In that uncertain interlude between light
and dark, time stretches   extends the likeness
of the opposite shoreline further and further
into the lake smooths its surface
until barely undulating, the water creates
an imperfect mirror.

Unhurried, the sun dips
casting fall colors across treetops. Orioles
whistle   sail from branch to branch
where they are made fluorescent
in the remaining sunlight.

Sky blends pale blue to dazzling cobalt.
Suddenly a lamp is hung high
above the water.   Someone names it
a blue moon, as it spreads
a glittering path across the dark
surface of the lake.

—Pat Magnuson

High School

The officers would prance around naked
in the locker room after drill team practice.

Debra Sue, a lieutenant who was
one of my rivals, liked to demonstrate

how she shaved the backs of her legs.
She'd be doing *splits* at the same time,

and we'd all watch, stupefied.
This was in the days when girls

swept their hair up into rubber bands
and rolled them around orange juice cans.

For some, it straightened their hair.
For others, it left a little dent in their foreheads

like they'd had a lobotomy.
While doing high-kick routines to

We're from Big D, my oh yes,
I'd wander outside the line to observe.

There was a stranger in my place
who smiled like me,

was out of breath from jumping,
and wouldn't be caught dead

wearing an orange juice can.
At my high school reunion

I met one of the orange-juice-can-wearers
at the door. She looked like she'd been

stopped in time, had travelled to Mars
or something. She kept repeating,

I'm single and like to mingle,
as though her brain had been plugged

to electrodes in the orange juice can.
My old boyfriend says that the only reason

for attending a high school reunion,
is to sleep with someone

who rejected you years ago.
Later on, he disappeared into a noise

of 70s rock with single/mingle.
I heard a movie star joke on TV,

that if she ever won an award,
instead of thanking people

she'd expose by name all the girls
who were mean to her in high school.

Wouldn't the list be too long?
Like that roster called out at 7:00 a.m.,

as drill team girls stepped onto dying grass,
grilled by sun, Old South cans.

—Carla Hartsfield

Nightshine

She was here inside the purple-eyed daisies
and honeysuckle lining the fence—

arriving seconds after visiting the moon,
her starched, white dress

cascading from frothy clouds—
but even more white like the light

that is said to emanate from reverence;
everything she touches extols circumference,

cool gowns and day lilies, wings
that have never taken flight but need to,

unsure feet touching windy stretches of sand—
she believes that she's guiding us through

the fragile terrain of complex thought,
like flowers lit from within beneath

a sky so transient, visions must be stolen
from nightshine and magnified against infinity;

she is here to tell us that real illumination
lives in the space between

wrong rhyme and wronged hearts, noting
these spaces glow with phobic energy—

an element causing her diminutive form
to whisper and hide,

rather than lose immortality
to the unknown Master—

in the twenty-first century,
unless we are privy to nightshine

and the genius of white flowers
in humble yards,

or we stumble across unexplained light
lingering over the rosemary and lavender—

we should pay more attention to our
earthbound heaven; someone, maybe Emily,

is showing us how to transcend,
bloom beyond recognition.

—Carla Hartsfield

For the good-bye

When the hour of the dream arrives
and sad they lock me in my solitude,
I want you to know:
That the sun will rise above the land
where our love lights up
for the daily given
of this country that sings freedom.

For that hour, without fears or happiness,
I have all the verses prepared,
will be the moment, as the day that I was born,
of an universal song and you will hug me
opening your soul to keep my bones
as a nymph that waits for the tender winds
that will take me time after time
to all the *tambos* where love is kept
and you will smile.

This communion from ever and forever
It will make my skin your skin,
song of *quena*, of monkeys and rivers,
the wind that rocks the tree of life,
extending me on pampas and Andes,
from one sea to another, among warm sands
or blue waters where the sky
it is still drawn clean, waiting for the wind
to cry the river that, ananconda, will draw
my name into your skin.

—R. A. Chávez

Tambos: Hostals
Quena: Inca's pan flute

Lost words

The child
with eyes open wide
sees a man beating a woman
and cries,
the world paints the past,
seeding desperation and anguish.

The mother kisses the child
and promises love forever,
singing cradle songs
to an innocence already broken
in the lights
of the morning's lost words.

The father is a silence that breaks
in the night of the city
between beer and dancing silks,
hides himself in a prayer
thrown in the face of the world.

The promises are winds
that can't hold the heart.
The child
runs, runs, runs. . .

—R. A. Chávez

Word and algebra

The morning
explodes in all the voices
and opens the doors of the alphabet.

World without father or mother,
just paper and pencil.

Sunny morn in autumn
that separates us from home,
to answer all our questions.

As the prodigal son
I walk toward her,
She waits for me with her books
to deposit the magic
of the word and the algebra.

Good-bye mom,
the winds are taking me away
from your breast and love.

Life seizes in her classroom,
to the son of your soul.

—R. A. Chávez

My father isn't home

The door is closed.
My father isn't home.
He leaves with his silence
to look for bread
or perhaps to seek his freedom.

He left behind
his woman and his child,
pulling himself into the day,
dragging his faith,
inventing his smile.

He is life's miracle
reflected in the lights
of a cold morning
that doesn't shelter his years.

My father goes away
and my steps follow him.

—R. A. Chávez

Homegrown Roses

Everyone has a story to tell
that's set inside a bar. I remember
the long year I loved a boy from school,
how every day at five o'clock we met
at the Red Door, how we became familiar,
the aging lady bartender calling
out in her clear voice—*Miller, Miller Lite*—
before that big door eased shut behind us.
I also recall being conscious
of the clock, how in the world of the tavern
you are always alive in the future,
even if it's only ten or fifteen
minutes, long enough to know the baseball
game you're watching is behind you, that if
you hope hard enough your team can still score,
there's time and plenty of it. Imagine,
too, one chilled summer night when I was young
and fleeing my first divorce, found myself
at the End of the Trail in Dayton, Nevada.
I met a man who bought me drinks, who fed
the jukebox till I thought it would burst,
held me close enough to hear his heart.
I don't remember when we decided
to pretend—this is a bar story,
after all—but we told the other patrons,
four tired cowboys and a black-eyed woman,
that we'd just been married, this was our
honeymoon and we were happy.
One of the cowboys wandered outside,
broke a rose from a battered bush, placed it
in a beer bottle, a gift for the bride.
I still have it. And now every year or so,
when I return to my truck in the dark

after work, I find a single rose anchored
under the wiper. My friends think I should
be afraid of this, as if this flower
were a dead chicken or a stalker's sad song.
But it's just a rose and all it means
is that I'm forever married to a man
who'll never know my name, who I couldn't
possibly pick out in a crowd.
Now you go. Tell me one of your stories.

—Gailmarie Pahmeier

Home Cooking

What I'm about to tell you is true.
It was in the paper some few years back,
but I'd forgotten until you asked
about my sister, asked if I thought
she was a pretty baby, asked if I'd
taken good care of her. The answers are *yes.*
She's the one with the rich red hair, my father's
clear grey eyes that can be blue, can be
startled into green. But that's not the story
I wanted to tell you. Here's what happened:

Somewhere in Florida a young woman worked
the counter at Bubba's Bodacious Bar-B-Q,
worked hard because she had a pretty
baby, a daughter she hoped would one day
ease into beautiful. People said, *that sure
is a pretty baby,* and she believed
them, too much a mother to own that that's
just what polite people say. She heard
tell about a children's beauty pageant
coming to town, and this could be her child's
ticket, but entry was fifty bucks
and how's she to get that when all she did
was wrangle ribs apart for customers
who never heard of ten percent. Now Bubba's
doing good, she figured, kept an extra
cash box. So late one night after all were gone,
she carried the big knife, the one Bubba
sharpened while he chewed and spit,
she carried this knife into the back dark
and jimmied open that box for fifty bucks.

I'll bet all that money shined with promise,
with the pure beauty of opportunity.
She can't remember hearing Bubba's footsteps,
how he came up behind her, how she turned,
and the knife, the big knife, sunk right into him.
What she'll always remember is how she
stood there in his blood and clutched twenty
dollar bills into nests, how she knew then
her daughter would never be beautiful,
would always hunger for the wrong things:
a boy to bring her a bag of blueberries,
his long, hard kiss, her heart wrapped in his hand.

Does this answer your questions? *Yes,* my
sister is both lovely and dangerous,
and *yes, yes,* we did the best we could.

—Gailmarie Pahmeier

On the Inside Looking Out

The clock on the factory wall
seems to be broken.
Tick,   tick,   tick.
Employees with vacant eyes
stare form their posts,
flies trapped in amber.

    Outside a breeze
    rattles dried leaves
    across the parking lot.
    They spin, children
    playing with the wind,
    running for the horizon.

Inside, the world shrinks to one
small room. Cracked concrete
walls resemble trade routs
on an ancient map.
Routs no longer viable
to cities long dead.

    Outside, an endless azure dome
    arches overhead, held up
    by four clouds, the corners of the earth.
    A formation of geese in flight
    assert their presence, midway
    between Washoe and Pyramid.

Inside, banks of florescent tubes flicker,
three out of every four burnt out.
Vacant workstations pushed
together in small puddles of light.
The darkness concealing
the lack of productivity.

—Timothy Michael Rhodes

The Perils of Home Ownership

Carrying twigs, tufts of hair
and dry grass in his beak,
a green tail towhee swoops
under the porch awning
and up into the rain gutter.
His mate, a puff of tan feathers
hides in a purple cloud,
the blossoms of a tamarisk tree.
For two years
I've watched them
build nest after nest
only to be destroyed by wind
or neighborhood cats,
leaving them bereft of eggs.
He sits on the porch railing,
brown and black feathers fluffed
and stares at me,
singing his challenge.
She flutters down to examine
his work with a critical eye.
I hear them scratching
on the aluminum gutter,
imagine him telling her
all of its virtues:
It's solid and secure.
No cat will reach us here.
She flies back to the tree
as if unconvinced.
He continues to build,
flower petals, bits of newspaper,
a wire twist tie,
an avian dream house
doomed by the first
thunder storm of summer.

—Timothy Michael Rhodes

Midnight in the Super K

The exhaust fan on the dairy case
taps a bossa nova rhythm.
Orange bell peppers and cactus leaves
pair off in a sensuous Tango
while fluorescent lamps hum
a wordless accompaniment.

A handful of bachelors push
carts up the aisle from
sportswear to produce,
voiceless ghosts who haunt the night
with nothing to do but squeeze melons.

Canned music echoes through
deserted departments
making the silence louder,
blotting out the memory
of laughing children,
playing hide and seek
amid the racks of discount jeans.

Pimple-faced youths stack boxes
in the aisles to restock for the day.
At the checkstand a man,
silent shadow in casino black and white
waits for a cashier. In his cart
a half dozen eggs
two raisin bagels
and a quart of cheap beer.

—Timothy Michael Rhodes

Counting Grains of Sand

Today we take inventory,
   neatly stack boxes,
   like children rearranging our toys,
   tape shut the open ones
   and write the quantity on the outside,
   2000 screws, 1876 nuts, 562 bolts.

The numbers march
   across scraps of paper,
   ciphers in an unknown equation,
   words in an foreign alphabet,
   a hymn no one wants to sing
   to the god of futility.

Shelf by shelf we count and date
   ranks of cartons and empty shelves.
   What are they doing with the numbers?
   No hose, zero valves, out of tanks.
   Same as yesterday.
   Same as tomorrow.

The Arabs invented the zero,
   to be a place holder
   when nothing is present.
   A circle of unity embracing
   all that is and will be,
   a hole in the center, our future.

—Timothy Michael Rhodes

A Drink like Gentlemen

for Col. Julius Raith, 43rd Illinois

Fill your canteens, boys! Some of you will be in hell
before night, and you'll need water!
> —Col. Isaac C. Pugh, 41st Illinois
> April 6, 1862 Shiloh, Tennessee

Hell rose up to meet us that day with the morning smell
of bacon and coffee, the omen sun barely risen red
over the river. Mist silvered like premonitions in the cattails
and through the blossoming peach trees. Men hung laundry

to dry on the bushes and blacked boots for inspection.
The Rebs wouldn't attack us, encamped as we were
on the banks of the Tennessee. They settled in at Corinth,
we thought, and were waiting for us there. So strong

was Grant and Sherman's belief we didn't bother
to entrench. We had ignored the evidence—the pickets
we encountered and skirmished. Green yet
in the 43rd Illinois, we saw the fight as Mister

Lincoln said—strained bonds of affection, someday
to sing again in Union chorus touched by the better
angels of our nature. We saw no angels
there that day. First the shots echoed through

the ravines. Then came the word and with it
metal rain. Cecesh balls tattered flesh before
we could answer the assembly drum. We scrambled
to fight the onrush of gray. They were not

men, I had to think, no angels here; they were
demons with Harpy voices—part Cerberus,
part screaming woman, part roasting damned
soul. Rebel yells that stopped me in my boots,

and hesitated my finger to reply. They were the enemy
we had to fight and kill or die ourselves. When
Sherman's Fifth fell back, the gray attack
focused all they had left on us—later they

said eight thousand Rebs against our brigade, but we
didn't count. We thinned their ranks with obstinance
and bullets. Then we were ordered to fall back to defend
the Purdy-Corinth crossroads. Sherman on one side,

driven back. McClernand's 29th on the other, driven back.
"Hold the line," Colonel Raith commanded. We held
and answered shot with shot. We and the 17th
were last to hold the crossroads. Three cannon were

ordered to retreat; two galloped off but all the horses
on the third were shot; screamed louder than a
woman. Men dragged that cannon off. Then
the 17th with ammunition nearly gone called retreat. We

held—that is—until a Minie ball shattered Raith's right
thigh, exposed the bone. I couldn't see the angels, blinded
like Phineus, my world befouled with the acrid salt and
smoke of gunpowder, the rain of blood soaking dirt

into mire. Then we had to drop back too, retreating over
a corduroy of comrades fallen in the mud. We tried to
carry the colonel with us to the rear. He couldn't dam
the cries of pain and told us then, "put me down, boys.

You'll do the cause more good by holding off those Rebs."
In the ravine we laid him in the shade under a tree. I turned
to fight. Shrapnel rained, cut through, turning red the blue
of my sergeant's uniform. I fell, one more plank in the bloody

road. Lucky it was, hard metal slicing through hip
flesh rather than the lead hell of a Minie that would
have taken bone. I could no longer walk. But I could
crawl. Raith, under the tree, fifty feet away. Down

the ravine to him over the path of dead and dying
souls. They say the road to hell is paved with good
intentions. I know better now. I saw the paving there that April
morning in the gory mud they called the place of peace.

I reached him soaked with sweat and blood. His breath
came soft; his eyes gems of pain. "Charlie," he said,
"If you can make it back, tell them where I am. But don't
stay here with me. It's too close to the fight." I leaned

against the tree with him and said, "I can't go any farther.
I'll stay here with you." I pulled a flask of whiskey
from my breast pocket, poured a little into my wound
to burn and ease. I offered it to the colonel; he did

the same. Saved half for later. The sun shone hot that
afternoon; we heard the battle rage beyond us; charge
and retreat and yet again. The setting sun shone red
on the stygian sight. The colonel closed his eyes. Quiet

we listened to the cries of wounded men for
water, for help, perhaps for death. The smell of
blood drew hordes of wild pigs to feed on fallen
men-a sight I'd never want to see again; yet only

death will let my eyes forget. I shot a few to stop them;
more came than I had bullets. I stayed awake that night,
clubbing them off with rifle butt as far as I could reach. God
answered cries for water; it began to rain, then wouldn't

stop. We shared what body heat we had. Rain drowned
it soon enough. Near dawn the deluge stopped. Then light
filled the sad ravine and the battle drew again. The pigs
were gone; I dared not view the sight they left behind.

Through heat and smell we waited, drifted, until the fighting
stopped. I offered him my whiskey—this time he drank, and
said "When we get home, we'll go downtown. We'll share
a drink like gentlemen." I drank. The litter

bearers found us late that afternoon. I didn't get to say
good-bye, but wished him well. They carried him to Pittsburg
Landing, and took his leg aboard the steamer Hannibal.
He died four days later from his wounds. I healed; went back

to fight again on other fields. Now that the war is over,
on April 6th I walk downtown and stop at Kaesbach's
Saloon. I buy two drinks—two whiskies—one for the Colonel
and one for me; and we share a drink like gentlemen.

—PF Allen

Your Son Asks for Prayers
for Paul Millmann

So I pray you into a sparrow
just leaving Venus' arms
with the fruit of the tree of the knowledge
of love, flying as we cannot yet fly
toward November. Twenty seven, 27,
the day you'll die—
the two with its vacant open eye twisting away
from the gentle, one-winged seven.
Here are the symbols for November,
the dark strokes of prayer that pull down
the clouds and part them at your feet.

All morning the dog has barked at the tree.
So I pray you into a dog,
enthralled by leaves and sap and wings,
and how the moon descends and swings
its pendulum there in the empty arms
of the gumball tree
bending and tapping away your time here.

Let me pray you into a tree,
grey, its fingers holding sky,
as you hold only sky
in that hospital bed, your eyes closed
to the soft-soled, sparrow hearted nurses,
the dog lowering it's face to the earth,
the tree's pulse slowing
as the sap descends.

And you hanging on for something,
numbers, prayers, clouds,
the memory of birds,
or maybe the deer that crossed your path,
all muscle and hair and breath and heart
pushing through the cold autumn sky,
that last morning before you knew
about deer, how they'll take you
on their backs and you can almost
smell the scent of animal death—
taking you somewhere vibrant and green—
the trees, maybe.
Yes. The trees.

—Donna Biffar

Little Shavers

Imagine them as saviors
disposed in the rubble
of toilet paper rolls,
cotton balls and used pads,
those sharp-toothed nazis
grinning as you open
the medicine chest. Salvation
is only for the hairless—
as Adam and Eve were
on that first day before they knew
how sexy
fur is. Imagine
Yahweh sending little shavers,
two by two,
pink for girls, blue for boys,
their slick, disposable legs unridged by sin,
parading past the fountains,
the hair of prairie grass,
bamboo, exquisite trees—
to eradicate all trace
of fish with tufts, with legs,
to slash the blacks and Jews,
the poets who snuck in.
And they march
Yahweh's march,
legs straight, dropping.
Adam and Eve practice,
and Adam is better. True,
He could've struck them
shagless. But what good is will?
The shavers manufacture handsome rows,
the winds of evolution snaking through

their sharp jaws. See the sea,
the lungfish traipsing up the beach,
the dinosaurs sprouting feathers,
the chimps descending.
Eve pets the little shavers,
kisses their foreheads,
and alpha male Adam caresses her legs,
her apple flesh
so tempting
he doesn't part the hair
to bite.

—Donna Biffar

Three Murders In Winter

The yellow lilies you brought me
are just now beginning to lose their fire
and yesterday I removed the two red roses
for hanging, although you've told me you hate
the display of dead flowers.
It's a northern custom to punish color.

*

You've seen this streak in me before
the morning you came back to the bedroom
in my red satin robe, your hair spilling
like cornsilk over your shoulders.
I stripped you down with nervous laughter
and called you ridiculous.
The cold, it gets in so deep.

*

The lilies will not, they will not
submit to embalming. And for this
they are guillotined between my thumb
and forefinger at the first sign of weakness.
Yellow stigmata on my palms
here's the smell of it still.

—Kyran Pittman

Boy Waiting for Snow

a painting by Johnny, age six

It could come
out of the blue
spontaneous sky
the fleckless firmament
that saturates the paper
with cerulean possibility.
It could come, falling
flakes like starry cobwebs
no two alike, not ever.
Boy's tongue poised to tell
each from each.
Boy's face
(circle, line, dot)
shining certitude.
Boy's round head transcendent
buoyant as a balloon bobbing at last
into the stratosphere.
Anything could happen from here.

—Kyran Pittman

Blondie

In Mexico they called you guerra
tongues clicking like castanets
in their chestnut faces
the shawled and venerable flower ladies
turned wanton, beckoning lasciviously
as you'd approach
the old men in the *jardin* braying
toothlessly in your wake
young toughs taunting
schoolgirls giggling
pandemonium
everywhere you went.
Not even in our own bed were you safe
your yellow hair between my thighs
the riot cresting in my limbs
a voice from my throat
calling "guerra, guerra"
and laughing softly.

—Kyran Pittman

If He Were to Ask What She is Thinking

I have been here before. At midwinter
weary of dimmed restaurants and shaded windows
we came along backroads to this very place. The trees
were bare then and it seemed my eye could cut
an infinite path between them, the forest floor
etched out in stark precision, veiled now
by the blind of green that shimmers diffuse
in the pollen drenched rays of this spring afternoon.
But that day the light was low and piercing
and I ached with the nakedness of it all
like ice caught in my throat and melting slowly.
And now that I think of it, that was the last good day
we had together. See how everything has grown in.

—Kyran Pittman

American Jericho

there are words for this, there is a language we speak
that
can embrace this
             define this
                      explain this

lead us out of this

but we have not used it
and we must

the guilt I feel is intense
                      about the joy I get

reading of the weather underground
or of the armed struggle at wounded knee

the guilt I feel is intense
                      about the inspiration I get

listening to the stories of huey on 63rd and adeline
or to the fuck the police bass of nwa

the guilt that I sympathize with terrorists and have to
                      explain this to my children

what are those words I must share
and I must
        must
             share them

we do not need to reinvent, to rediscover, to redefine our
                           lives or our language

we simply need to be honest and use what has been in
                              front of us for 500 years
truth justice and liberty for all
truth justice and liberty for all
for all

for the brothers and sisters in new york
for the mothers and sons in dc
for the fathers and daughters in the middle east
for the gente in south
for the lovers in our beds
for the people on our block

truth justice and liberty for all
armed with these words
no buildings will fall, no blood shed, no bellies empty,
                              no land occupied,

and like mohammed to mecca we will come home at last
                              circling clockwise seven times
and reciting our hellos, our good-byes, our quiet words
                              of pain and remorse, of
forgiveness and redemption

and we must
must
speak these words,
pick up this rubble
resurrect ourselves
speaking into being monuments
that nothing can topple

—Tom Moniz

poem for the inauguration of the president

this is just a poem
just one poem
meaningless, harmless
but if I
pass it out
again and again
if I put it up with your sign
if I pave the way of your protest with it
or
if I wrap it around your linked arms for
their protection from the police
or cover your mouth from the slowly
gathering gas
or
if I cradle your rock
slingshot style
in it
or push it against
your bleeding body
and soul
to keep the blood in

if I do that

watch
just watch
as people become nervous
cities crack down on dissenters
police look to hassle civilians
governments fear their subjects
presidents hide in motorcades and white houses

but why should they worry
for this is simply a poem
just a poem from me to all of you

—Tom Moniz

after reading some lines of Charles Wright, I make my way to the back yard

to think about the
stillness of places
the landscape of my
life in the now:
the children, the women
and men,
the meals cooked and counters cleaned
endlessly
domesticity ad infinitum
and it's hard to see a way out
or through
the things that keep you from the stuff you love:
your body, this life, this child and that one,
the morning I wake to see all of us in bed;
the stillness of those moments
is a spirituality unrivalled,
enough to make a man like
me drop what I feel I must do
must, must do,
and sit for a minute,
in the moment,
and watch the way this fly lands here and then there
and hear the way my child laughs and then falls back into silence
and the way it all slips into perfect order
a still-life
full of life—
mine.

—Tom Moniz

Lost Ending

Right now, in a town where you have never been
and will never visit, they are filming a movie,
which you will not see, with actors you haven't
heard of, with one exception—the star, a fine-boned
actress with a face like a violet, whom you admire intensely.
When the movie comes out, you do not
hear about it. It is an independent film,
and the month it hit the art house,
you had papers to grade, an account to land,
a case to work on; it was tax season.
Other people, some of whom you know, will see
the film and admire it, intensely.
Over dinner they discuss the lush
garden imagery, the vision of Paradise glimpsed
in the foliage, of the remarkable performance
of the fine-boned actress. After one such
conversation, a girl whom you do not know
will walk, wistful and fine-boned, through her blooming
apartment late at night, admiring the soft
invitations of African violet, the blown-back
delicacy of cyclamen, the brassy plumpness of
her philodendron. If you were to meet her, you would
fall in love: she is funny and vulnerable,
wears mismatched socks and forgets Tuesdays, which
would charm you dreadfully, take your breath,
until you decided, abruptly, that it was an artifice.
You would leave her on the corner, her hands full of
leaves and flowers, on a grey day.
The director calls cut. You return to your trailer.
She returns, slowly, to her own.

—Sonya Wozniak

Search, Call, Arrival

Like gold mining in the clod-packed, hard-scrabble self,
seeking the ore you can smelt to song,

or like a man in the grim city, calling his dog,
calling endlessly, his voice twisting like a lasso,
and the Great Dane of muscled sound, power in its
haunch, comes or not, as he pleases—

poetry, when it deigns to heed, tears the air,
forcing the wimpling invisible to palp to its wing—

like a hand extruded from a rocketing car,
pushing against the low hard sky,

which is just how your weight crushed me, pressed
me flower-flat, forcing my enthralled, ball-tossed heart
into a stiff wind.

You, the dog: muscled haunches, a spill of gold,
confusions of desire, song, and arrival.
Even in sordid sheets, my ghost comes singing:
a fainting word miser who occasionally
(much like you) comes, when called.

—Sonya Wozniak

What was I thinking?

A card turns;
the moving moon blew cold music
at. The noise of a cat. The light of tunes
bounces from the silvered ruff.
Whatever this night is: Enough.

Next day,
no one had any notion of hydrangea
or tinsel stars. The engine turns over.
I am slightly hysterical; you have
come upon me; we must start the car.
Quickly to get away.

No one here forever
the bird still calls out: moonlight,
moonlight, moonlight. Never.

—Sonya Wozniak

Wherein I Come to the Sudden Realization That I Am Celestially Disliked

Why does the sky hate me?
Why is its eye so blue and liquid-brimming with invective?
I dissolve into the sidewalk against the might of its wide,
unpupiled iris.

When the ocean dislikes you, avoid the beach.
When the sky hates you, the rooftops
aren't strong enough to hold back its vast disdain.
My buckle spine and sad crown plea for mercy:
be clement, I beg, be temperate and mild, but
storm lurks even on a clear day, and I hear
its hiss-tongue warning:
I know I am little, and despised.

—Sonya Wozniak

Loving the Light

My mother and I went downstairs,
and I thought of you.
Hearing the washer run was like your heart.
My mother, looking at your seat
where you would do bills.
When the light flickered my brother yelled:
there is no light to lead us.
Then the washer stopped.

—Becca Stroh

The Eagle I Saw One Day

Her eyes were the color of the sun.
Her feathers golden like the desert.
Her beak orange like the changing leaves.
Her claws as sharp as a misspoken word.
Her wings glide through the sky
and I on her back.

—Austin Scofield

Contributors

PF Allen is the editor of the poetry journal *Moon Reader*, published by Snark Publishing, and is poetry editor of *The Midday Moon*. Her chapbook, *The Homeless Man Eats Ice Cream,* was published in 2001 by River King Poetry Press. A full-length book of poetry, tentatively entitled *Answering the Moon,* is pending publication by Bellowing Ark Press.

Pam Alvey has been a special education teacher in Reno, Nevada. She has also worked as a ferryboat captain in Saugatuck, Michigan, a speech and language pathologist, and a guide in a marine museum. She is a member of the Ash Canyon Poets and co-editor of *The Ash Canyon Anthology.*

Walter Bargen has authored eight books of poems. The most current title is *Harmonic Balance* (Timberline Press, 2001). He is co-editor of the anthology *Rising Waters: Reflections on the Year of the Great Flood.* His poems have appeared in over one hundred magazines.

Elinor Benedict won the 2000 May Swenson Poetry Award for her collection, *All That Divides Us (*Utah State University Press). She has also published five chapbooks of poetry and several short stories. She is an M.F.A. graduate of Vermont College, and served as founding editor for *Passages North* literary magazine.

Donna Biffar is the author of two books of poetry, *Water Witching in the Garden* and *Events Preceding Death.* A chapbook, *Down: and Other Syndromes* (2002) was published by Pudding House Publications. Her next chapbook, *When Tractors Are Art,* is forthcoming from Snark Publishing. She edits *River King Poetry Supplement* and Southwestern Illinois College's literary magazine, *Head to Hand.* She is a co-editor of *New Century North American Poets* and the upcoming River King Poetry Press anthologies *The Black Angel,* and *The Best of River King.*

R. A. Chávez was born in the Hacienda Gallinazos district of Puente Piedra, Lima, Peru. He is the founder of the pamphlet *Epoca* (poetry) and has studied in the poetry shop at ANEA (The National Association of Writers and Artist) with Carmen Luz Bejarano, Juan C. de la Fuente, Eduardo Adrianzen, Cèsar de Maria and others, and has worked with the Ash Canyon Poets. He is a winner of a Nevada Arts Council Fellowship for the year 2001-2002.

Peter Christensen has published poetry and essays internationally in magazines, literary journals, and anthologies. His latest book is *Winter Range* from Thistledown Press.

Leonard Cirino lives and works in Springfield, Oregon. He is the author of 23 chapbooks and collections of poetry from 14 presses. His collection, *The Terrible Wilderness of Self,* from Cedar Hill Publications, was nominated for the National Book Award in Poetry, 1998.

Tony Clark lives in Georgetown, Texas. He has been writing for more than 40 years. His works include poetry, fiction, articles, essays, and dramatic works.

Earl Coleman had a lengthy career as a publisher then turned to writing full-time about ten years ago. He has been published widely (poetry and prose), and nominated for Pushcarts XXIII and XXVII for short stories. He has published one book of poetry, *A Stubborn Pine in a Stiff Wind* (Mellen Poetry Press, 2002).

Bill Cowee lives in a small town near Reno and works as a chief financial officer for a wine and spirits distributor. He is a founding member of the Ash Canyon Poets. He has one book, *Bones Set Against the Drift* (Black Rock Press).

Philip Dacey is the author of seven books of poetry, the latest *The Deathbed Playboy* (Eastern Washington University Press). Widely published in periodicals and anthologies, he teaches at the Minnesota State University in Marshall and has presented readings and workshops in half of the fifty U. S. states and several foreign countries. Awards include two NEA fellowships, three Pushcart Prizes, and a Fulbright Lectureship in Yugoslavia.

Chip Dameron's fourth collection of poems, *Greatest Hits*, was published in 2001 by Pudding House Publications. He lives in Brownsville, Texas, where he teaches writing and literature at The University of Texas at Brownsville.

Paul Dilsaver's (1949-2002) novel *Nurtz! Nurtz!* is an underground, cult classic. He was a prolific writer, of poems, short stories, reviews and novels. Some of his poetry titles include *Malignant Blues, A Brutal Blacksmith, An Anvil of Bruised Tissue, Character Scatology, A Cure for Optimism, Medi-Phoria, Hardcore Haiku, Book of Tears* and *Encounters with the AntiChrist.*

Terry Forde has spent 25 years in radiology. She is a member of the Ash Canyon Poets in Carson City, Nevada.

John Garmon's poems have appeared in *Ploughshares, Prairie Schooner, Southern Poetry Review, River King Poetry Supplement, Southern Humanities Review, Atlanta Review,* and other journals. He is the sponsor and co-editor of *New Century North American Poets.* He is president of Vista Community College in Berkeley, California.

Dana Gioia is a poet, critic, and literary anthologist. Author of *Can Poetry Matter?*, he is a frequent commentator for the BBC. His most recent volume of poetry, *Interrogations at Noon* (Graywolf Press, 2001), won the American Book Award.

Shaun T. Griffin lives at the Western-most edge of the Great Basin with his wife and two boys. His last book of poems was *Bathing in the River of Ashes* (University of Nevada Press, 2000).

Craig Hadden, a former community college English professor, now serves as dean of instruction at Vista Community College in Berkeley, California. A native and long-time resident of Colorado, he lived in Arizona, Texas, Pennsylvania, and Germany before making the move to the West Coast in June, 2002. While in Germany, he performed as a singer/songwriter in folk clubs and folk festivals.

Ray Hadley was born Evanston, Illinois. He lives at Lake Tahoe, California where he owns Keynote Used Books and Records. He has one chapbook, *Smoking Mt. Shasta* (Blackberry Press).

Jim Harris' books include several poetry chapbooks, a volume of the annual publications of the Texas Folklore Society, and a ranch history. He is a past president of the Texas Folklore Society. For over six years, his column "The Southwest" appeared weekly in the *Hobbs* (New Mexico) *News-Sun*. He has worked as a photojournalist and a writer since retiring from teaching in colleges in Louisiana, Texas, and New Mexico. In addition to writing and publishing, he is director of a county historical museum in Lovington, New Mexico.

Carla Hartsfield was born in Waxahachie, Texas, immigrated to Canada in 1982, and until recently taught piano in the Glenn Gould Professional of the Royal Conservatory of Music, Toronto. She is a singer/songwriter and self-taught autoharp player. Her third major poetry collection will be published by Brick Books (London) in 2003. In 2002 she was the recipient of two senior-level writing grants from both the Canada Council and the Toronto Arts Council.

Robin Elizabeth Holland received her MFA in Poetry from Vermont College in 1990. She lives and teaches in Maryland. Her poetry has been published widely in literary journals, anthologies, and magazines.

Richard D. Houff is the editor of *Heeltap Magazine* and Pariah Press. He has written a novel and five volumes of short stories that are currently unavailable in the USA. His poems, plays, and essays have been published throughout the world.

William Kester taught and directed plays in community college for more than 20 years. He is presently retired and lives in Oakland California.

Michael Kiriluk is an expatriated Californian living in Nevada where he is a member of the Ash Canyon Poets.

John Knoepfle is the author of 17 books of poetry, including *Poems from the Sangamon*, *Begging an Amnesty*, and *The Chinkapin Oak*. In 1986 he received the Mark Twain Award for Distinguished Contributions to Midwestern Literature. He is currently preparing a new manuscript called *Prayer Against Famine and Other Irish Poems*.

Peggy Sower Knoepfle is married to poet John Knoepfle. Her publications include a book of poems, *Sparks from Your Hooves*, and a collection of essays, *After Alinsky: Community Organizing in Illinois*. She has visited Nicaragua and Colombia with Witness for Peace and is on the board of the Auburn Food Pantry and the Mary Wood Branch of Women's International League for Peace and Freedom.

Mary Sue Koeppel's first book of poetry was *In the Library of Silences, Poems of Loss* (Rhiannon Press 2001). She is the longtime editor of *Kalliope: a Journal of Women's Literature and Art*. She edited *Lollipops, Lizards, and Literature* (1994) and co-edited *Women of Vision, An Experience in Seeing by the Visually Impaired* (2000). She is the winner of the Esme Bradberry National Contemporary Poets' Prize (Wordart), an Art Ventures Grant, and the Frances Buck Sherman Award, and has had three Pushcart nominations.

Ted Kooser's most recent book is a collection of personal essays, *Local Wonders; Seasons in the Bohemian Alps* (University of Nebraska Press, 2002). His most recent book of poems is *Winter Morning Walks; One Hundred Postcards to Jim Harrison*, from Carnegie-Mellon University Press. He is a retired life insurance executive who lives in rural Nebraska.

Wayne Lanter is the founder and co-editor of *River King Poetry Supplement* and River King Poetry Press. He has published four books of poetry, *The Waiting Room, Threshing Time: a Tribute to James Hearst, At Float on the Ohta-gawa* (Honorable Mention from the Edwin Mellen Poetry Press contest on a book-length poem commemorating the bombing of Hiroshima), *Canonical Hours,* and a novel, *The Final Days,* is forthcoming. He is a co-editor of *New Century North American Poets*.

Charles Levendosky has authored 10 books and chapbooks of poetry. His first book, *Perimeters*, was published by Wesleyan University Press in 1970. *Circle of Light* was published in 1995, and Clark City Press is scheduled to print his next book of poetry, *The Peeping Tom Poems*. In 1988 Levendosky was appointed Poet Laureate of Wyoming, a position he held until 1996. In 2000, the Wyoming Arts Council awarded him a Literature Fellowship, and *Prairie Schooner* literary magazine honored him with its Edward Stanley Award for Poetry. Levendosky has been editorial page editor of Wyoming's statewide newspaper, the *Casper Star-Tribune,* since 1982. His weekly column appears on the *New York Times* wire. He is widely recognized for his First Amendment commentary.

Lyn Lifshin has written more than 100 books and edited four anthologies of women writers. Her poems have appeared in most poetry and literary magazines in the U.S.A., and her work has been included in virtually every major anthology of recent writing by women. Winner of numerous awards including the Jack Kerouac Award for her book *Kiss The Skin Off,* she is the subject of the documentary film "Lyn Lifshin: Not Made of Glass." Her latest books are *Cold Comfort* and *Before It's Light* (Black Sparrow Press). Another book, *A New Film About a Woman in Love With the Dead* is due out soon.

Joanne Lowery's most recent collection is *Double Feature* from Pygmy Forest Press. She has published in numerous magazines and journals. She lives in Michigan.

Anne Macquarie was born in Yosemite Valley and now lives in Carson City, Nevada, where she is a member of Ash Canyon Poets

Pat Magnuson was a member of the Ash Canyon Poetry Group of Carson City, Nevada. She has co-founded the Red Oak Writers group in central Minnesota. Her work has been anthologized in *90 Poets of the Nineties.*

Jo McDougall is the author of four books of poetry. The latest, *Dirt*, was published by Autumn House Press, Pittsburgh. She is the recipient of a DeWitt Wallace/Reader's Digest Award, an Academy of American Poets Award, Arkansas's Porter Fund Literary Prize (2000), and others. She lives in Little Rock.

Chuck Miller has published nine books of poetry: *A Thousand Smiling Cretins, Crossing the Kattegat, Hookah, How in the Morning, Oxides, from Oslo-a journey, Harvesters, Thin Wire of Myself,* and *Northern Fields.*

Philip Miller serves as the art editor of *River King Poetry Supplement* and is a co-editor of *The Same*. He is on the board of directors of the Writers Place in Kansas City, Missouri where he directs the River Front Reading Series. He has published poems in various magazines including *Poetry, Georgia Review* and *Rattapallax*. He is a co-editor of *90 Poets of the Nineties* and is the author of four books: *Cats in the House, Hard Freeze*, and *From the Temperate Zone.*

Pete Mladinic lives in Hobbs, New Mexico. He was born and raised in New Jersey and has lived in the Middle West and the South of the United States. He was enlisted in the United States Navy for four years and received an MFA in Creative Writing from the University of Arkansas in 1985. His poems have been published in numerous literary quarterlies such as *American Literary Review, Puerto del Sol, MSS, Poetry Northwest,* and *Poetry East*. He teaches English at New Mexico Junior College.

Tom Moniz lives in northern California. He teaches at Vista Community College, Berkeley, California.

Gailmarie Pahmeier's literary awards include the Chambers Memorial Award, a Witter Bynner Foundation Poetry Fellowship and two Artists Fellowships from the Nevada Arts Council. Her most recent book is *The House on Breakheart Road* (University of Nevada Press, 1998).

Kyran Pittman is from Newfoundland and lives in Little Rock, Arkansas.

David Ray's books include *Demons in the Diner, Kangaroo Paws, Wool Highways, Sam's Book* and *The Maharani's New Wall*. A memoir and a book of poems, *One Thousand Years—Poems about the Holocaust,* are forthcoming. He lives in Tucson with his wife, Judy.

Judy Ray is author of two books of poetry, *Pebble Rings* and *Pigeons in the Chandeliers,* and a prose memoir about India, *The Jaipur Sketchbook: Impressions of India.* She is co-editor, with David Ray, of *Fathers: A Collection of Poems.* Other poems, essays, and photographs have appeared in many publications, including*: New Letters, Paterson Literary Review, Sonora Review, Flyway,* and *Hampden-Sydney Poetry Review.*

Timothy Michael Rhodes was born in Honolulu, Hawaii and raised in Hayward, California. He now lives in Reno, Nevada and is a member of the Ash Canyon Poets.

Austin Scofield is the oldest of four home-schooled children. *The Eagle I Saw One Day* was inspired by a day fishing with his dad at Moose Lake in Alaska.

Michael Seltzer lives and writes in Sparks, Nevada. His poems have appeared in *The Beloit Poetry Journal, The Antigonish Review* and other literary magazines. He is a former editor of *Bristlecone,* and is completing an MFA in writing from Vermont College. He is a member of the Ash Canyon Poets.

Yvette A. Schnoeker-Shorb works as co-publisher/editor of Native West Press and is a mentor for Prescott College. Within her poetry she attempts to emphasize that "the hardest part of being human is the immense self-consciousness because with it comes enormous responsibility to the 'others' who extend biologically beyond the reach of our anthropocentrism and to the Earth that endows humanity with existence."

Glen Sorestad is from Saskatoon, Saskatchewan. He has over a dozen books of poetry to his credit, the most recent being *Today I Belong to Agnes* (2000) and *Leaving Holds Me Here* (2001). His poems have been anthologized in more than 40 anthologies and textbooks. He co-founded a literary publishing house, Thistledown Press, and retired from publishing in 2000 after 25 years of publishing. Sorestad is a Life Member of the League of Canadian Poets and in 2000 was appointed the first Poet Laureate of Saskatchewan.

Becca Stroh is a seventh grade student and the winner of the 2001 and the 2002 St. Louis' Bi-State Development Agency and Arts in Transit Program's poetry awards for St. Louis metropolitan area grade and high school students. She has read her poetry on various television shows and at the Brewhouse Theatre in Somerset, England.

William T. Sweet is a native Oregonian who teaches at Lane Community College in Eugene, Oregon. He leads workshops for advance placement high school and gifted junior high school students. His poetry has appeared in various journals in the U.S., Australia, Iceland, France and the Philippines.

Sonya Wozniak teaches at Vista Community College in Berkley, California.

Stephen Caldwell Wright is founder and president of the Gwendolyn Brooks Writers Association of Florida, Inc. and is a member of the National Planning Committee for the Zora Neale Hurston Festival of the Arts and Humanities. He is the author of two collections and 10 chapbooks of poetry. His poetry and fiction have appeared in numerous publications, including *The Colorado Review, Phylon,* and *The Carolina Quarterly.*

Anne Ohman Youngs has three poetry chapbooks: *Markers, A Bracelet of Mouse Hands,* and *Thirty Octaves Above Middle-C.* Her full-length book, *Template for Break Dancing,* is due out from Northern Michigan University Press later this year. She is a charter member and former editor of *Passages North* literary journal. She currently lives and writes in Battlement Mesa, Colorado.

Acknowledgements

PF Allen: "A Drink Like Gentleman" appeared in *River King Poetry Supplement* and *City Primeval*. Reprinted by permission of the poet.

Elinor Benedict: "Two Women Leaving Beijing." Reprinted by permission of Utah State University Press. "A Daughter-in-Law Watches the Old Man Hesitate." Reprinted by permission of March Street Press.

R. A. Chávez: "For the good-bye," "Lost words," "Word and algebra," and "My father isn't home" are reprinted by permission of the poet.

Leonard Cirino: "Another One for Jeri" appeared in *The New American Imagist*. "Letter to Jeri After Waking from an Erotic Dream" appeared in the *Lummox Journal* and the *New American Imagist*. Reprinted by permission of the publishers and the poet.

Tony Clark: "My Wife Among the Apaches" appeared in *New Texas 2001*. Reprinted by permission of the publisher and the poet. "The Forest Park Zoo Caper" was published in *Literary Fort Worth*. Reprinted by permission of TCU Press and the poet.

Earl Coleman: "Eleven In the Sticks appeared in *Aura Literary Review*. "Busting Out" appeared in *Thin Air*. Reprinted by permission of the publishers and the poet.

Philip Dacey: "The Ice Cream Vigils" appeared in *The Kerf*. "Doozy" appeared in *The Midwest Quarterly*. "Four Hands" appeared in *Poetry International*. Reprinted by permission of the poet.

Paul Dilsaver: "Disconnected" appeared in *Nerve Cowboy*, in the on-line source *B.G.S.U. Alumni Anthology*, and in the collection *Book of Tears*. "Alignment" appeared in *Writers' Forum* and in the collection *Medi-Phoria*. "Garden Lie" appeared in *Pulpsmith* and *Character Scatology*. "Corwin Psychiatric Ward" appeared in *Open Places, Poets West, Sutured Words* and *Malignant Blues*.

John Garmon: "Autumn Drunk" appeared in *88 Journal*. Reprinted by permission of the publisher and the poet.

Dana Gioia: "Words," "Elegy with Surrealist Proverbs as Refrain," "The Lost Garden," "New Year's" appeared in *Interrogations at Noon* (Graywolf Press, 2001). © 2001 by Dana Gioia and reprinted by permission of the poet.

Carla Hartsfield: "High School" was published in the collection *Fire Never Sleeps*. Reprinted by permission of Signal Editions/Vehicule.

John Knoepfle: "saint brigids well" appeared in *The Shop*. "all hallows for sam hain" appeared in *New Letters*. "dancing with the inupiaq" appeared in *Illinois Times*. "on flat top mountain: lines for a miscarried child" appeared in *The Other Side*. Reprinted with permission of the publishers and the poet.

Peggy Sower Knoepfle: "This Smoke of San Judas" appeared in *River King Poetry Supplement* as "Barrio San Judas." "Clothes Hanging on a Line" appeared in *Illinois Times*. Reprinted by permission of the publishers and the poet.

Wayne Lanter: "Watching Her Die" and "Tragedy" appeared in *Moon Reader*. Reprinted by permission of the publisher and the poet.

Lyn Lifshin: "*Kiss*, Baby, the New Film" appeared in *A New Film About a Woman in Love with the Dead*. Reprinted by permission of March Street Press and the poet.

Pat Magnuson: "Big Bang Poetry" appeared in *River King Poetry Supplement*. Reprinted by permission of the poet.

Chuck Miller: "Time, " "Over and Again You See Them at the Pool," and "Extra Virgin" appeared in the collection *Crossing the Kattegat*. Reprinted by permission of Mica Press.

Philip Miller: "Snow's on the Way" and "Isis and Osiris" appeared in *Poem*. Reprinted by permission of the publisher and the poet.

Gailmarie Pahmeier: "Home Cooking" and "Homegrown Roses" appeared in *Rio Grande Review*. Reprinted by permission of the publisher and the poet.

David Ray: "Preparing the Monument" appeared in the anthology *September 11, 2001: American Writers Respond.* Reprinted with permission of Etruscan Press and the poet.

Judy Ray: "Counting the Bats" appeared in *River King Poetry Supplement*. "Ghazal" appeared in *Friends Bulletin*. Reprinted with permission of the publishers and the poet.

Becca Stroh: "Loving the Light" originally appeared as a part of the St. Louis' Bi-State Development Agency & Arts in Transit program.

Glen Sorestad: "Kvikne in Rain" has previously appeared in *The Norseman*. "Dreaming My Grandfather's Dreams" has appeared in the on-line journal, *It's Still Winter*. Reprinted by permission of the poet.

William T. Sweet: "Fire Watch" is a part of a manuscript entitled *After the Fall* which won a 1994 Oregon Literary Arts poetry fellowship.

Anne Ohman Youngs: "Something Like Those Mice" first appeared in the collection *Thirty Octaves Above Middle-C*. Reprinted by permission of Wind Publications and the poet.